BANK MANAGEMENT

By

Walter Kennedy

President

THE FIRST NATIONAL BANK
MONTGOMERY, ALABAMA

BANKERS
PUBLISHING
COMPANY
BOSTON

Bankers Publishing Company

BOSTON

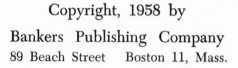

This book is affectionately dedicated to the late Harold Stonier, former Executive Manager of the American Bankers Bankers Association, and the Founder of the Graduate School of Banking, whose personal friendship and activities in furthering banking education have been an inspiration to this author for more than thirty years.

WALTER KENNEDY

Preface

The procedures and techniques in the management of a commercial bank will inevitably depend upon the volume of assets of the bank which will, in turn, determine the size and degree of specialization of the staff.

While fundamental principles and policies of banking may be much the same in banks of all sizes, it is obvious that the duties and problems of the executives of a large metropolitan bank will be quite different from the duties and problems of the officers of the small, two or three man bank.

Somewhere in between these two extremes is the medium sized bank, which is the backbone of the American banking system. This text is devoted to the management of a medium sized bank since it is impractical, if not impossible to prepare such a text that will be equally applicable to banks of all sizes.

This immediately poses the question—"What is 'a medium sized bank'?" A number of appropriate yardsticks might be used for this purpose, namely:—the amount of deposits, capitalization, total resources, gross income, etc., but for a number of reasons, the number of employees is believed to be the most practical measure of size.

For the purposes of this text, a "medium sized bank" is considered to be a bank with from twenty-five to five hundred banking employees. Any bank with fewer than twenty-five employees might truly be considered a small bank, and one with more than five hundred employees is certainly a large bank.

Most of the author's experience has been with banking institutions in the middle brackets of the limits suggested. It is recognized that in the very small banks and in the large

v

metropolitan institutions, the policies, procedures and problems herein discussed, would, in many instances, not be applicable.

The medium sized banks, as herein defined, embrace a large number of banks, perhaps five thousand, located in every state of the Union.

To discuss fully and adequately the subjects embraced in this text would require virtually a complete book on the subject of some of the chapters. In fact, complete books have been published on several subjects which are discussed. It has, therefore, been impracticable to go into detail on many phases of the subject matter. Where a subject has been more fully treated in some authoritative book, reference is made to such text, in case the reader seeks further information.

In the larger and medium sized banks, bank officers may be classified into two groups, the "generalist" who is concerned with all phases of bank management and the "specialist" who is concerned with only certain departments or certain phases of bank work. This book is prepared for the generalist, or perhaps the specialist who would like to know more about other areas of banking, perhaps with the idea of becoming a generalist at the executive level.

The specialist in any department will perhaps not find his special subject fully treated here but he will probably find much concerning other departments that will be new to him.

The principal objective has been to provide bank executives and potential executives with some sound principles, policies, and procedures on each of the major activities in a medium sized bank. So far as can be learned no previous book has achieved this.

Much of the material has been assembled by the author in a search for the solution to practical problems which existed in his own bank.

There has been an attempt not to repeat or paraphrase material that has been adequately covered and well stated in other banking publications, but this is an effort to outline principles, methods, and procedures that have been learned by actual experience and observation, and sometimes by mistakes and trial and error.

The various functions and departments of banking have been approached, not with the objective of giving detailed instructions in those functions, but rather to express a sound viewpoint and philosophy of management with respect to such matters.

The author is indebted to his colleagues at The First National Bank of Montgomery who have reviewed the subjects in which they are particularly interested and have offered many helpful suggestions which have been incorporated in the text. He is particularly grateful to Elizabeth Dickerson, his secretary for the past twenty years, for typing and retyping the many drafts of the manuscript.

It is hoped that the opinions, observations, philosophies, and studies of a banker who has spent most of his adult life in a medium sized bank, will be of some interest and help to the executives, present and future, of this large segment of our American banks.

PREFACE TO SECOND EDITION

IT IS OF course extremely gratifying to an author to have his book achieve widespread acceptance. The need and demand for a book at the executive level on the subject of Bank Management is evidenced by the sale of all copies of the first edition in less than twelve months after publication.

While the book was written primarily for bank executives, potential executives, and directors, the surprising fact developed that it attracted the interest of other groups. One of the better known Eastern universities adopted it as a textbook for its advanced class in banking and other schools of commerce and business administration are also using it.

In preparing the second edition, an attempt has been made to include material concerning some recent banking developments. Among the banking subjects of great current interest are—charge account service plans, and check credit plans. A new section has, therefore, been added to Chapter VIII discussing these relatively new forms of installment credit.

Chapter XX on the subject of Bank Directors, has been rewritten and amplified to cover some important phases of director relationships.

Other new inclusions in the revised edition are a suggested form for a statement of investment policies, a revised statement of loan policies, a plan for progress reports on all bank employees, and a revision of the portion of Chapter IX, dealing with real estate appraisals.

It is the hope of the author that the revised edition will continue to serve a useful purpose in banking literature.

June 1959   WALTER KENNEDY

PREFACE TO THIRD EDITION

ONE OF AN author's more pleasant tasks is the writing of a preface for a new edition for the reason that it indicates that there is still a demand for the book.

When the manuscript for *Bank Management* was written some five years ago, the author had no motive other than to share with his contemporaries in banking some of the fundamental principles of banking which had been learned the hard way, through research, and trial and error.

In reading through the book in preparation for the publication of the third edition, the author was acutely aware that much of the material was elementary in character and would perhaps seem trite truisms to bankers of wide experience in that particular area. On the other hand, very few bankers are well informed in all banking functions and perhaps even the experienced banker can find the book useful to fill in some of the areas in which his experience has been more or less limited.

Perhaps the most startling developments in banking during the past decade have been in the field of automation. Electronic Data Processing is a subject that no progressive banker can ignore. While the subject is complex to the extent that a complete book or perhaps several volumes might be required to treat the subject exhaustively, the fundamental principles that a bank executive should understand can be reduced to a chapter.

The new chapter on Automation in Bank Accounting, which appears as Chapter XII in the third edition, is the result of approximately five years of research and study by the author and some of his associates in The First National Bank of Montgomery in the process of selecting and installing an electronic data processing system in the said bank. The manuscript for this chapter was also checked and approved by representatives of one of the larger manufacturers of electronic data processing equipment.

Chapter XXI, on the subject of Bank Mergers and Consolidations, was inspired by a Bank Management Seminar sponsored by The American Bankers Association in Washington, D. C., in November, 1962. Dean James Hayes of Duquesne University School of Business Administration, one of the leaders of the Bank Management Seminar, was very helpful in the preparation of this chapter.

Chapter XXII entitled "The Bank President's Role" is largely the result of a talk on that subject delivered by the author in May, 1962, at a meeting in Winter Park, Florida, sponsored by The Florida Bankers Association. This chapter, to some extent, summarizes the activities of a Bank President with reference to all of the aspects of Bank Management mentioned in the other chapters.

While each passing year brings new developments and innovations in banking procedures, the basic principles of Bank Management appear to remain stable and enduring.

WALTER KENNEDY

June 1963

Table of Contents

CONTENTS

CONTENTS

CHAPTER I

Organization Principles

THE WORD "MANAGEMENT" is susceptible of many definitions. (A definition that seems particularly applicable to bank management is: "Management is the art of getting work accomplished through the organized efforts of other people.")

Bank management encompasses activities in many different areas, and medium sized and large banks are subdivided into many different departments and divisions. In the broadest sense, however, bank management can be divided into at least three more or less separate areas or phases, namely:

1. Economic.
2. Technical.
3. Human Relations.

In the field of economic problems bank management is concerned with an understanding of and an analysis of existing business and economic conditions, as well as probable future trends. Such an understanding is necessary to the formulation of plans and policies in both the investment field and in the area of lending and business planning.

The technical phase of bank management is largely concerned with methods, procedures and matters of internal operation and control.

While the economic, technical and human relations aspects of bank management are frequently inter-twined and dependent upon each other, it is believed that the higher echelons of bank management are more often concerned with the human relations phases than the economic and technical phases.

Among the more difficult duties of a bank chief executive is selecting, training and directing department heads, or, as someone has expressed it, "managing the managers."

One of the primary duties and responsibilities of top management is "to divide up the work." Therefore, it is logical that one of the first matters to be considered in undertaking the management of a bank is: What is to be done? And next, who is to do it?

A visual presentation is often helpful in formulating a plan or in explaining the relationship of a number of associated functions. In recent years, a schematic arrangement known as an "Organization Chart" has been widely used as a tool of administration or management. Large corporations with complex organizations for a long time have found organization charts helpful to a complete understanding of the relationship of the various departments, divisions, and sections to each other.

The military services have likewise used various types of organization charts to delineate lines of authority and responsibility. Thousands of Americans serving in the armed forces within the past generation have gained familiarity with organization charts in the military or naval service.

Most banking textbooks which deal with administration have used organization charts to illustrate both departmental organization and the overall corporate structure.

There are a number of different types of organization charts. Some of them deal solely with functions, while others use names or titles without functions, and others use names, titles, and functions. The Army uses a type of organization chart called "Authorized table of strength" which indicates the various ranks and grades of personnel (and sometimes equipment) for the units under consideration.

There is almost a complete lack of uniformity among banks and bankers as to titles and functions. The duties and functions performed by the Vice President and Cashier in one bank, may all be assigned to an officer designated as the Comptroller in another bank of equal size, and this same principle is true of most bank titles. A medium sized bank may have eight or ten officers who bear the title of Vice President, and yet the duties and functions of each of them may be widely different. This is also true of other conventional bank titles.

The principal functions of any commercial bank logically fall into a few major groups. In a medium sized bank the principal functions may be properly classified as:

1. Lending.
2. Investments.
3. Accounting and Banking Operations.

In addition to these major functions, there are others such as General Administration, Auditing, and Business Development. A large number of medium sized commercial banks exercise trust powers and in many such banks trust business is a major function. Other medium

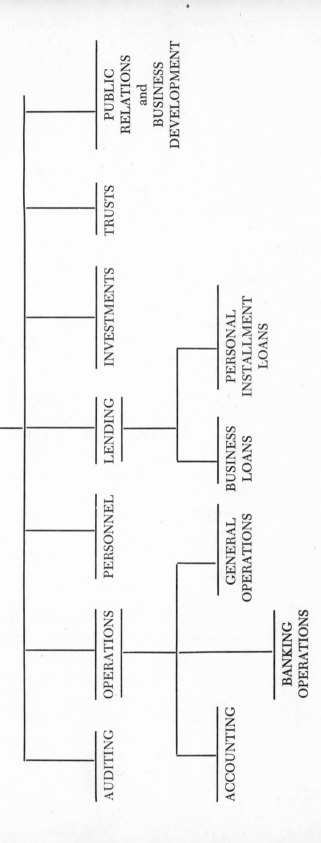

CHART I

FUNCTIONAL CHART

GENERAL SUPERVISION

AUDITING • OPERATIONS • PERSONNEL • LENDING • INVESTMENTS • TRUSTS • PUBLIC RELATIONS and BUSINESS DEVELOPMENT

OPERATIONS: GENERAL OPERATIONS

GENERAL OPERATIONS: ACCOUNTING • BANKING OPERATIONS

LENDING: BUSINESS LOANS • PERSONAL INSTALLMENT LOANS

sized banks may have Foreign Departments and Travel Departments.

Having decided to prepare an organization chart for a particular bank, the decision must be made as to whether it is to be merely a functional chart, or whether it is to indicate the duties, responsibilities and functions of individual officers and department heads. In most cases, the last mentioned type of chart will be more useful, but for purposes of illustration, both types of charts are shown for the same institution.

Chart I is purely a functional chart without attempting to relate functions to individuals. Chart II is an organization chart showing the allocation of duties, responsibilities, and functions to the various officers of the bank.

Chart III is another type of bank organization chart which might be used in the personnel office to indicate the job titles in each department and the authorized number of positions in each section.

Perhaps the greatest benefit that can be expected from an organization chart is the assurance that each officer in the bank will have a definite, written outline not only of his own duties, responsibilities and lines of authority, but also for every other officer. The mere act of compiling an organization chart will sometimes disclose that there is not a clearcut division of authority, responsibility, and duties.

It is seldom that a newly organized bank is either a medium sized bank, or a large bank, and most medium sized banks result from the growth of a small bank or result from consolidations or mergers.

Organization charts are particularly helpful in the case of mergers to clearly delineate functions and responsibilities.

Most small banks are essentially "one man banks" in

the sense that one man assumes primary responsibility for all the phases of management. However, when a bank progresses to the point where one man cannot keep up with all phases of the operation, it becomes necessary to departmentalize and delegate functions and responsibilities. It is at this point that organization charts become particularly helpful.

· Many a bank has suffered because the chief executive has not recognized early enough that the size of the operation has passed the point where one man can effectively supervise all details.

Any officer, upon assuming the position of Chief Executive of a sizable bank, should prudently study the organization chart if one exists and if there is no such chart, he could make no wiser beginning than the preparation of such a chart for his own guidance, as well as for the benefit of his associates.

It is not the purpose of this chapter to attempt to tell bank executives or potential executives how the duties or functions of a particular bank should be grouped or allocated. Often an organization has to be shaped and built around the characteristics and capacities of the people who are then available.

An organization set-up which may be entirely appropriate with a particular group of individuals, may be entirely impractical if other individuals are substituted. Duties, responsibilities, and functions, therefore, must be shifted from time to time to meet changed conditions and changing incumbents. An organization chart should, therefore, be a flexible device which must be changed to meet changing conditions, rather than something sacred to which individuals must be molded to conform. The chart is merely a record of the duties, responsibilities, functions, and lines

6

of communication which the management has decided to be the most prudent under existing circumstances.

Outlined below are some broad general principles which should be borne in mind in planning the allocation of duties and responsibilities in a bank:

1. Avoid undue concentration of authority and primary responsibility in any one person.
2. Avoid dual or multiple bosses as far as possible.
3. Prohibit overlapping authority.
4. Delegate authority to act to the lowest expedient level.
5. Keep all functions in proper perspective.
6. Be sure that appropriate authority accompanies responsibility.
7. Make clear the appropriate lines of communication and make such channels as simple as possible.
8. Limit immediate supervisory control to as few people as possible.
9. Don't hesitate to change the organizational set-up to conform to the capacities and limitations of individuals.

An organization chart in itself has no particular value, but behind it is evidence that management has a clear, concise understanding of:

1. What is to be done.
2. Who is to do it.

The communication of this understanding from management to the staff is the principal function of the organization chart.

Another manner of cataloging the overall functions of the management of a bank might be outlined as follows:

1. To provide plans and policies.
2. To supply and maintain an adequate staff of properly trained people.

3. To supply appropriate quarters and the necessary physical equipment.
4. To provide adequate training, direction and supervision.
5. To maintain effective two-way communication throughout the organization.
6. To exercise control through appropriate reports, checks and balances, audit procedures, and personal leadership.

There may be other phases of bank management but they can probably be appropriately grouped under one of the broad categories outlined above.

CHAPTER II

Manual of Procedure

MOST LARGE METROPOLITAN BANKS
and many medium sized banks use a manual of procedure
to describe standard operating methods and procedures.
Such manuals are sometimes called "Manuals of Operations" or "Operating Manuals" instead of Manual of Procedure.

A satisfactory definition of an operating manual is: "A
bank operating manual is a written statement of standard
operating practices prescribing the operations of the bank
as a whole, as well as the operations of each department
and sub-department".

Banks use a number of various types of manuals, some
of which are similar to operating manuals, but should not
be confused with the typical manual of procedure. For
instance, many banks use Employee Handbooks, or Staff
Manuals to describe personnel regulations and working
conditions. While a section might be devoted to this purpose in a manual of procedure, a staff handbook or staff
manual, which deals with personnel matters only, is not an
operating manual. Some banks publish one or more man-

9

uals described as policy manuals which contain an outline of management's policies dealing with certain subjects. For instance, some banks have a policy manual dealing with lending policies. Another such manual might be devoted to investment policies, but a statement of policy only which does not outline standard procedures for operations would not be considered an operating manual. In some banking organizations, instead of issuing a manual of operations, standard practice bulletins are issued from time to time and such instructions remain in effect unless superseded by later bulletins. Training bulletins or training manuals which describe operations down to the minutest detail may be employed by banks for training purposes but in the typical manual of operations it is not usually necessary to describe operations in such great detail as might be employed in a training manual.

Some of the larger banks have one manual of procedure which applies to the bank organization as a whole, and separate departmental manuals for each of the major departments. However, in a medium sized bank it is usually preferable to have one manual of procedure which covers the entire bank with separate chapters and sections for the various departments.

Six principal reasons may be cited as the purpose in preparing and maintaining a manual of operations for banks.

1. To find "the one best way" to perform each operation within the bank.

2. To prescribe the "one best way" for each operation and maintain it as a standard procedure to be followed.

3. To obtain uniform methods of performance both

within a given department, and between various departments.

4. To provide an aid for training new employees.

5. To provide a reference book which may be considered authoritative as to how any operation in the bank should be performed.

6. To improve the overall efficiency of the bank's operation.

The Armed Forces provide a classic example of the use of manuals of procedure. The military forces use regulations at every level to prescribe in detail how administrative procedure shall be carried out. Industrial and commercial organizations have also used manuals of operation to some extent and in 1938 a survey of 240 medium sized, and larger banks, showed only 1/4 of them were using manuals of procedure, however, out of 19 New York City clearing house banks, 17 of the banks were using such manuals. During recent years the use of operating manuals by banks has been discussed and taught at such banking schools as The Stonier Graduate School of Banking, Rutgers—The State University, New Brunswick, N. J., and the School of Banking of the South at Louisiana State University, and as a result of many banking students' receiving instruction in operating manuals at such schools, there has been a widespread increase in the use of such manuals.

The question is often asked, "What size should a bank be to profitably use a manual of procedure?" It appears that in any bank where the operating officers are not in close personal contact with all operations, either because of the number of employees, the number of branches, or a lack of sufficient operating officers, a manual of procedure is needed. It has been pointed out that in small banks some-

11

times most of the knowledge of operating procedures is confined to some one key man. If the standard procedures are reduced to writing, this will serve as a protection against the loss of the knowledge of the principal operating officer. After all, the fundamental difference between a large bank and a small bank is largely one of volume—not of scope.

A typical Manual of Operations in a medium sized bank might be expected to contain the following sections:

1. A statement as to the functions and use of the manual. (Explanation to user.)
2. A chapter containing:
   The history of the bank (desirable, but not necessary.)
   An abridgement of the portion of the bank's by-laws, which pertain to the operation of the bank.
   An organization chart showing the grouping of the bank's functions and the allocation of responsibilities.
3. A statement of the general policies of the bank with respect to:—Public relations, accepting new business, personnel regulations, etc.
   (The first three sections might also appropriately be included in a Staff Hand Book.)
4. A section devoted to general operations affecting more than one department, such as the handling of mail, telegrams, telephone service, stenographic procedures, purchases and supplies, preservation and destruction of records, advertising, security measures, etc.
5. The largest portion of such a Manual would be devoted to banking operations. This portion should include a detailed description of each sub-department and section, such as the General Bookkeeping Depart-

ment, Paying and Receiving Tellers, Proof Department, Individual Bookkeeping Department, Statement Department, Savings Department, Collection Department, Safe Deposit, Safekeeping, Loan & Discount Department, etc. Each such section should contain a description of the functions performed and the purpose of such functions, the detailed manner in which the daily operations are carried out, with a list of "do's" as well as "dont's".

6. The operations of each other department of the bank should likewise be treated in a similar manner to the banking operation departments as described in Paragraph 5 above. In a medium sized bank, sections of the Manual would cover such departments as Trust Operations, Investments, Loans, Auditing, Business Development, etc.

The compilation of an operating manual for a bank is a very sizable task that would probably require many months, and should not be entered into without a full realization of the amount of work involved. The principal expense will be the indirect expense of the time spent by the bank personnel assuming the responsibility. The direct expense of mimeographing, multigraphing, or printing the manual and placing it in appropriate looseleaf binders will depend upon the number of pages (probably 300 to 400 in a medium sized bank), the number of copies and the type of binders used.

The compilation of a manual should not be undertaken unless it has the full support of top management since it will require the participation and cooperation of a great many people and the announcement and assignment of responsibilities should come from the chief executive.

The preparation of a bank manual of operations is

largely a matter of assembling or compiling rather than a writing job by one person. It should preferably be handled by a committee of officers of broad experience, who will review and edit the procedures as prepared in the various departments. The editorial committee should be headed by a senior officer who will have the authority and prestige to obtain cooperation throughout the organization in preparing the material.

The first step of the editorial committee should be the preparation of an outline or table of contents of the various sections to be included in the manual. The committee should then decide upon the various persons who are the best qualified to prepare the initial draft of each section and sub-section. It is well to decentralize these assignments as far down the scale as possible.

Once a decision has been reached to compile a manual, and the method of procedure has been decided upon, top management should make an announcement stating the purpose of the manual and outlining the procedure to be followed.

Following this announcement, the editorial board should call a meeting of each person who is to be assigned the task of preparing the initial draft of any part of the manual. At this meeting the matter should be thoroughly explained, and the assignments distributed to the participants. A time schedule should be established, setting dates for the return of the initial drafts to the committee. This is important so that the people involved will not procrastinate. It is also desirable to have a uniform flow of initial drafts reaching the committee each week rather than have all drafts submitted at the same time.

Some bank operating manuals are written in narrative style with complete sentences. Others are written in outline form. The style is not important provided that if written in outline form, it is complete enough to convey a clear meaning as to what is to be done and how.

While it is desirable to have all chapters and sections of the manual more or less uniform in style, this is not imperative and it is understandable that some sections might preferably be in narrative style, and others in outline. The principal objective must be clarity.

It is to be expected that many of the initial drafts received by the committee from department heads will not be in satisfactory form and may have to be returned for amplification or rewriting. In other instances the initial drafts with minor corrections and editing may be approved by the committee as a final draft.

One of the valuable by-products of a bank manual of operations is the searching self-analysis that is necessary in the preparation of a manual. One banker has stated that even if the manual is thrown away when the compilation is completed, the process of preparing it is worth while in itself. The discovery and elimination of overlapping and conflicting authority is one of the beneficial results to be expected.

An operation manual is never finished for the reason that it is to be expected that procedures and methods are certain to change from time to time and the manual to have value and be authoritative must be kept up to date.

Once the final draft is completed, a system must be devised for keeping the manual abreast of changes that are certain to occur. A permanent editorial committee should be designated with the duty of approving any proposed changes in the manual and also the responsibility of reviewing the manual at intervals from two to three years to see if any sections have become obsolete.

In addition to the permanent editorial committee, some staff member, probably the Auditor or the officer responsible for the audit function, should be designated to see that the procedures set forth in the manual are being observed in all departments.

When variances are discovered, either the manual should be amended or the procedures changed to conform with the manual. Before changing prescribed procedures, the editorial committee should be certain that the proposed changes are desirable and worth while.

In view of the expectation that the manual will necessarily be amended from time to time, it is important that it be prepared in loose leaf fashion, preferably with pole binders or ring binders.

Sufficient copies of the manual should be prepared so that every officer will have a copy and every department, sub-department or work location will have a copy. It is desirable to have the manuals serially numbered and issued to individuals who will be responsible for the custody and for posting amendments when they are issued.

Some banks require each new employee to read the general sections of the manual which apply to the bank as a whole and also the section which applies to the employee's particular job.

While a manual of procedure is not a panacea for a bank's operating problems, many banks have found it a valuable device in determining and maintaining the most efficient procedures. To be of lasting value, however, the manual must be kept up to date and not allowed to become obsolete.

CHAPTER III

The Personnel Program

THE MOST IMPORTANT THING about a bank is the people who compose the bank's staff. Without an adequate number of the right sort of people with appropriate training, qualifications and experience, a bank cannot do a good job.

No matter how fine the building and equipment, nor how perfect the systems and policies, there is no substitute for an adequate staff.

The largest category of expense in operating a commercial bank is salaries; therefore, too much attention cannot be paid by management to the matter of adequate, well-trained personnel and the manner in which they perform their duties.

Customer good will is a valuable asset. A bank's employees, through their daily contacts with customers, are the ones who, for the most part, determine the quality of the bank's public relations.

Employee relations, like public relations, is not something that can be solved by hiring a staff specialist for that purpose. While in a medium sized bank there is a definite need for a staff member specializing in personnel work, top management has a responsibility in this respect that cannot be evaded or delegated. On the other hand, there are many phases of personnel relations which can and should be handled by staff members.

In the military service, there is a sharp distinction between staff and command. In the exercise of command, direct orders are given in the name of the person issuing the order. A staff officer is an advisor to the Commander, and issues no orders in his own name or upon his own authority. In this sense, a personnel director of a bank is normally a staff officer who advises and assists, but does not directly supervise any employees or give any orders (except perhaps to the subordinate employees in the personnel department.)

Comparatively few medium sized banks have separate personnel departments devoting full time to this function. The most typical setup finds the Cashier, the Comptroller or some other senior officer as the personnel director, with some one under his supervision maintaining the necessary records and perhaps conducting the interviews with employee applicants.

Larger banks are apt to have a separate personnel department headed by an assistant vice president or perhaps a vice president. It is desirable that the personnel officer be responsible only to the president in order that he or she will not be subject to departmental influence or bias and can maintain an objective view that will be beneficial to the bank as a whole.

The personnel program of a medium sized bank should include some effort in each of the following aspects:

Recruiting

Screening and testing

> Orientation
> Training
> Counseling
> Morale
> Exit Interviews

A few words may be appropriate on each of the above factors.

The term "recruiting" embraces all appropriate media for attracting capable, potential employees to seek positions with the bank. Literature, films, talks, and personal interviews at both the high school and college level are found by many medium sized banks to be necessary and desirable in getting good new employees.

The American Bankers Association and the Financial Public Relations Association both have films, sound slides, and other material designed to attract students to banking as a career. Some banks have found it helpful to prepare a folder for their own bank outlining the attractive features of the employment conditions. These folders are distributed to high school seniors and are also distributed to the bank's own employees, since the bank staff can be of considerable help in obtaining new employees.

Banks which maintain an executive training course for college graduates have found that in view of the large number of corporations seeking college seniors, it is necessary to send representatives to the college campuses if they expect to hire the top level graduates.

Some one in every bank should have the duty of receiving and interviewing applicants for employment. In many medium sized banks this is a full time job at certain seasons of the year. It must be realized that in the normal course of events not everyone who seeks a job in a bank has the minimum requirements. Other applicants may be well qualified, but no suitable vacancy exists at the time the application is received.

The manner and tactfulness with which applications are received can be very important to the applicant's impression of the bank. Even the applicants who cannot be used can be won as friends of the institution. The interviewing of employment applicants is therefore important and should be entrusted to personable people who are well qualified for this function.

At this point, it is appropriate to comment on the qualifications of a bank personnel director. Whether the director is a man or woman does not appear to be as important as whether he or she has the personal qualities of: ability to gain confidence, sincerity, sympathy, an interest in people, patience, an even disposition, a lack of nervous mannerisms and a sincere desire to be helpful to others.

Since an ever-increasing percentage of bank employees are women, there is considerable argument in favor of a woman personnel director. In such cases, it might be appropriate to have some male officer who is designated as Employee Counselor, or "Dean of Men" for the male employees.

The American Bankers Association, as well as a number of management consultants, have prepared aptitude tests which are useful in selecting employees. The A.B.A. clerical test is an aptitude test that is specifically intended for bank clerks and covers skill in handling and comparing figures, vocabulary, word usage, etc. Other tests are available which will show dictation and typing speed, dexterity on accounting machines, etc.

Still other tests are designated to show personality factors and other personal characteristics. The value of aptitude testing has been very well established in recent years and suitable tests offer a bank a great many advantages over the trial and error method. While such tests will probably not prove 100% infallible, in most cases if they are intelligently used, they will be found decidedly worthwhile.

The personnel department can perform a very useful purpose in a bank if it can screen the obviously unfit applicants through written applications, personal interviews, aptitude and personality tests and other such methods. Having selected the most likely candidates, the final selection and hiring in most cases will be done by the department heads or immediate supervisors who will direct the new employee. Requiring a department head to take an employee whom he does not personally approve at the insistence of a personnel director or any other official is usually unwise. The personnel director can recommend, but in most cases should not make the final decision to hire.

Once the decision to hire has been reached by the supervisor involved, the personnel director can do a great deal in the orientation of the new employee. All of the details of the medical examination, the preparation of the personnel record forms, the surety bond application, the group insurance forms, as well as a general orientation talk and tour through the bank, should be handled by the personnel department. Many banks use a staff handbook to give the new employee information about employee rules and regulations, salary administration, vacations, sick leave policy, retirement benefits, etc. Such a booklet can be very helpful in this respect.

Some one should also be designated to look after each new employee on the first day of employment to make sure that he or she knows where personal belongings are placed, the location of the rest rooms, the customs with respect to recess periods, lunch hour, care of equipment, quitting time, etc. Instruction in such matters should not be taken for granted, but should be specifically assigned.

In one fairly large bank (250 employees), the President each month holds an orientation conference with all new employees hired during the preceding month. The conference lasts about an hour and is devoted to an outline of the bank's organization and an explanation of the function of each of the major departments. Considerable emphasis is placed upon the importance of the individual in his or her human relations, both with fellow employees and the public. The new employees are urged to ask questions, and frequently do so.

In the past, banks have largely depended upon employees learning by absorption with little formalized training. The larger metropolitan banks have learned by experience that formalized training can be effectively used to reduce the period of apprenticeship and standardize work performance. The training systems employed by the large city banks can, in many cases, be scaled down to fit the training needs of medium sized banks.

In every bank, regardless of size, someone should be conscious of and assume responsibility for training employees. In the very small bank, the responsibility will undoubtedly fall on the principal operating officer, whatever his title might be. In the medium sized and larger banks some staff officer should be assigned the duty of planning the various types of employee training that are needed and supplying the material for such instruction. Some of the instruction can perhaps be given by the personnel department, but some of it which may be somewhat technical in nature, can best be given by persons more familiar with actual operations.

The principal function of the personnel department in this field should be to determine what type of training is needed, and the best method of providing this training. Once this has been decided, it is management's function to decide how and who is to proceed with the execution of the various phases of training.

Some of the various phases of training that might be provided in a medium sized bank are:

1. Proper methods of using certain bank accounting equipment, such as adding machine, bookkeeping machine, proof machine, etc.

2. "Do's and dont's" for individual ledger bookkeepers.

3. Teller's procedures, including fundamental principles of negotiable instruments, and "do's and dont's".

4. Fundamental principles of supervising people.

Certainly any discussion of training in commercial banks should include mention of the courses of the American Institute of Banking, but this type of instruction should more properly be considered under the heading of banking education, rather than training for specific jobs. The A. I. B. courses should augment and complement the bank's training classes. It would be desirable if every bank employee could be required to take the A. I. B. course, "Principles of Bank Operations". If the local A. I. B. chapter does not offer the course, the person responsible for training in the bank should try to arrange for the course or its equivalent to be made available to the new employees of the bank each year.

Other A. I. B. courses, such as Negotiable Instruments and Commercial Law, might well be considered as prerequisites for promotion to such positions as paying teller, note teller, collection teller, etc. The personnel department should use its best efforts to encourage employees to take the A. I. B. courses which will aid in their advancement.

Banking education other than through the A. I. B. courses is available through the Study Conferences sponsored by many of the state banking associations and through the several graduate schools such as The Stonier Graduate School of Banking, Rutgers—The State University, New Brunswick, N. J.; The Graduate School of Banking at the University of Wisconsin; The Banking School of the South at Louisiana State University; The Pacific States Bankers School at the University of Washington, Seattle; and The Southwestern Graduate School of Banking, at Southern Methodist University, at Dallas, Texas. These graduate schools, of course, are for a selected group at the officer level who are potential top-flight executives.

The National Association of Bank Auditors and Comptrollers school in banking operations at the University of Wisconsin and the Consumer Credit School at the University of Virginia are also valuable for advanced training for specialists in these fields.

Every medium sized bank should have someone in the organization who is familiar with the various banking schools who recommends enrollment at these schools of appropriate persons from within the bank. Enrollment at such schools should be the result of planning by management rather than being left to the initiative of the individual.

In small banks the employees can usually confer with the chief executive on their personal problems as well as business troubles. This is hardly possible or practicable in medium sized banks. To some extent department heads may serve instead of the chief executive as an employee counsellor, but often times supervisors who are perfectly competent in other lines do not have the temperament or personality that fits them for employee counselling. In every bank there should be someone who is readily accessible, and who is fitted by position and personal qualifications as an employee adviser. The personnel director, whatever his or her title may be, should be such a person.

It is not practicable to attempt to prescribe specific personnel records for all medium sized banks. There are a number of variable factors in each individual bank that will make undesirable the adoption of standardized, uniform personnel record forms. However, there is certain basic information concerning the individual employees that should be readily available in every bank.

The needed information will include the employee's full name, date of birth, and personal history. All of the information of this type is usually included on an employment application blank. Therefore, the application should be retained as a permanent record. For employees of long standing where no such application was used, the form can be filled out for file purposes.

A folder or file should be maintained on each individual employee which will contain the employment application and all communications and data which affect the particular employee.

The employee's attendance record and time record (where such a record is maintained) should also be a part of the personnel folder. Any letters of commendation or criticism, together with a chronological record of all changes in duties, title, or pay and the application for surety bond, etc., will likewise be kept in the personnel folder.

In most banks, or any business organization for that matter, the problem often arises of persons who do not seem capable of advancing further beyond a certain level and therefore become discontented and unhappy. Unhappy employees can and do have an adverse effect on the attitude of other employees. The cause of frustrated and unhappy employees can arise from a multitude of reasons. Frequently it is because the employee is not equipped to progress further, or perhaps in some cases the employee is qualified and capable of further progress, but no opportunities for advancement exist.

The nature of the work in banks is such that there will inevitably be a large number of routine clerical jobs and a smaller number of supervisory or executive positions. If a bank should have a policy of only employing college graduates, it would necessarily follow that they would not be satisfied to remain very long in the routine clerical positions and the turnover would be very high. A portion of the new employees should therefore be persons without higher education who will be reasonably satisfied to hold a clerical position for several years at least. The best of these clerks should be trained and promoted to supervisory positions as they become available. There will necessarily be some amount of employee turnover in any business due to inevitable causes. A certain amount of turnover is normal and even desirable in that it prevents the same people remaining indefinitely on the same job which may be monotonous in nature and, unfortunately, in banks there are some jobs that are by nature monotonous.

One of the big problems that arise in many banks is what to do with the people who do not appear to have capacity or opportunity beyond the clerical or teller level. Some banks do not employ men except those who are believed to be potential officers. When they reach the age of thirty years, if it does not appear likely that there will be an officer's position available for them shortly, or if they do not appear qualified for an officer's position, they are released for other employment. This may appear to be a drastic way of handling the problem, but it is realistic and avoids having men reach middle age and become a problem because there is no further advancement possible for them.

It is understandable that many bank employees are perfectly willing to level off in a clerical, stenographic, or accounting position without supervisory authority, provided their salary continues to increase, but it is not realistic to suppose that a job will continue to pay more and more indefinitely for performing the same work. At some point, the maximum value of that particular job will be reached regardless of experience and efficiency. When the maximum is reached the employee must assume a more responsible position if further increases are to be earned and received.

More women seem to be willing to remain in routine positions than men and, for this reason, many banks hire women exclusively for the clerical positions in operating departments.

While women may be the answer to filling the clerical positions in banks, including the teller's functions, one of the biggest problems in banking is management succession and the development of capable officers for key positions.

The training and development of bank officers should be a definite program and not left to circumstances or chance. It is fundamental that if capable officers are to be produced there must be suitable material available to work with. As the general level of education throughout the country increases, it is desirable, but not mandatory, that officer trainees have the benefit of a college education. This is particularly true in the field of lending, investments, trusts, and public relations.

Nearly all of the large city banks, and many medium

sized banks, have a definite program of employing college graduates for training for officer positions. The usual type of bank officer training program consists of rotating the officer trainees through various departments for on-the-job training, with reading assignments and conference-type training classes. Some banks aim officer trainees at specific departments, while others maintain a group of trainees who are not intended for any particular department, but are available for any vacancies that may arise.

It is important that banks regulate the number of officer trainees to the extent that they will be able to absorb at the officer level, within a reasonable time, all of the trainees who show capability. It will be unfortunate, as well as expensive, to employ and train college graduates and then have them seek other employment because a suitable permanent assignment does not become available.

The American Bankers Association has done considerable research on the subject of executive development in banks and there is a liberal amount of literature available on this subject, as well as the closely related subject of management succession.*

Management which recognizes that there are many factors to motivate employees other than wages and properly applies these incentives, has the key to good employee morale. Surveys of hundreds of workers in practically every industry have indicated that the following are of equal or more importance than salary to employees:

1. Security.
2. Recognition that the employee is important to the organization.

---

*See: "Executive Development in Banking," published by American Bankers Association, and "Management Succession in Smaller Banks" by Wilbur H. Isbell, Graduate School of Banking Library, American Bankers Association.

3. Sincere interest in the employee's welfare and success.

An effective means of building employee morale is the wise use of praise. People need a word of encouragement now and then just as they need food. We pay salaries in money each month. We pay mental salaries by expressing appreciation for a job well done. Employees will work just as hard for mental salaries as for money. Money provides for our physical needs but mental salaries provide for our mental needs.

One method of enabling management to learn the employees' attitude toward their jobs and their opinions concerning the various phases of their employment is through an employee opinion survey. In 1950 Howard J. Morris, Jr., who at that time was an officer of The First National Bank of Montgomery, wrote a thesis for the Graduate School of Banking entitled "A Staff Conducted Employee Attitude Survey". The thesis is included in the Library of the Graduate School of Banking and also appears in condensed form in "Banking in 1950" published by The American Bankers Association. As outlined in Mr. Morris' thesis, such a survey can be conducted within the bank by its own personnel, but there are a number of management consultants who are experienced in conducting such surveys. There are some advantages in each of the methods, but in any event, it is important that if the results are to be considered authentic, the answers of the employees should remain anonymous.

Since the maintenance of a high state of morale should be one of the aims of a personnel department, an employees' attitude survey can be a useful tool of the personnel office in learning what the employees like and don't like about their jobs. Such a survey must be repeated every few years to keep up with the changing picture.

Another useful device in learning what the employees think about their jobs is the exit interview. An employee who is leaving the bank for any reason may be more willing to frankly discuss the employment conditions than an employee who wants to continue in the bank and is fearful of the consequences of criticism of working conditions. An exit interview to have any real value must be conducted under favorable circumstances by a skilled sympathetic interviewer, and the source of any criticism received must be preserved as confidential.

For management to be able to promote and maintain a high state of morale, it must understand and know what the employees are thinking. The personnel department should keep an "ear to the ground" and use all ethical and legitimate means for this purpose.

Communication between management and employees should be a two-way street and every effort made to expedite traffic in both directions. Suggestion box systems, regularly scheduled departmental meetings, occasional general assemblies, a bank magazine or newspaper are among the communications found useful by banks, but there is no substitute for a relationship between the supervisor and the employee which is based on mutual respect and permits a free and easy discussion between the two. It is also desirable that employees have the same type of relationship with executives above their immediate supervisors.

One method of communication from management to employees is through the medium of a bank publication. This may be in the form of either a monthly magazine or a weekly newspaper, and there are arguments in favor of both types. The weekly publication permits announcements while they are current and new, but a weekly requires proportionately more time and presents a number of difficulties. A monthly publication is more adaptable for the use of pictures and illustrations and can appropriately be larger in content.

In any event, a management sponsored bank publication should not be used solely as an instrument of propaganda or for "preaching" to the employees. If management's messages are to be received in a favorable atmosphere, other readable material must be included.

Periodical staff meetings are another potential channel of communication. In many banks the question of a suitable time and place for such meetings presents a difficult problem. If such meetings are to be successful, the environment should be attractive, the employees comfortable, and the acoustics satisfactory. A suitable assembly room which will accommodate comfortably all of the employees is something that few medium sized banks have.

Another difficulty with staff meetings is that on account of the staggered working hours of the various departments in most medium sized banks, it is difficult to find a time that is suitable or convenient for all departments.

The Wage-Hour regulations require that employer sponsored meetings must be counted as time worked. Such a meeting injected into a full work week will therefore possibly involve overtime. If such a meeting is held at a time when employees feel that they have other things to do that are more important (such as searching for a balance), the objectives of the meeting will be handicapped.

When they can be conveniently scheduled and held in suitable surroundings, employees' meetings are a splendid medium of communication. Sound films and slides can often be used to get an idea across visually more effectively than by a mere talk.

Banks have been leaders in supplying so-called "fringe benefits" to their employees. Such benefits as group life insurance, hospitalization insurance, retirement plans, profit sharing plans, employee lunch rooms, employee recreational and social clubs need no explanation here. Each bank should carefully study its own situation and determine what fringe benefits can appropriately be used. Bank management as well as industry generally has found such activities well worth the expense involved.

Retirement plans and profit sharing plans have become so important to banks that the next chapter is devoted to this subject.

This chapter on the personnel program would be incomplete if some mention were not made of association activities. In the banking field, there are a number of very fine associations which can not only render assistance to the member banks as corporate entities but can also aid in the development of individual bankers. Indeed the good work of these various associations is made possible through the unpaid voluntary participation of the hundreds of individual bankers who take part in these organizations. The principal associations are the state banking associations in each of the several states, the American Bankers Association with its various divisions and sections, including the Trust Division and the American Institute of Banking, the National Association of Bank Auditors and Comptrollers, Robert Morris Associates, and Financial Public Relations Association.

It would be desirable in every medium-sized bank for the officers to be encouraged to attend and participate in association activities appropriate to their particular field of interest. Where possible, the principal officer in a particular field (such as lending, operations, or trusts) should attend the national convention or meeting of the association in that field. In the event of state or regional meetings, perhaps junior officers as well as the department heads might be permitted to attend.

Attendance at such bank meetings not only informs the banker of current developments and makes possible valuable personal acquaintances with other bankers, but it frequently enables the banker to see his own problems in a different perspective when measured in the terms of the experience of others.

The associations mentioned above, and perhaps others, have a great deal to offer bank management and the best way to get the maximum benefit from such associations is through active participation by appropriate representatives.

CHAPTER IV

Retirement and Profit Sharing Plans

No OTHER FRINGE BENEFIT has received as much attention in recent years as Retirement and Profit Sharing plans.

Every bank executive should have an understanding of the basic principles involved in both retirement plans and profit sharing plans.

Practically every bank has a retirement plan of some sort, whether it is recognized as such or not. In many cases the plan is nothing but a more or less recognized policy that when employees reach an age which does not permit them to continue their former duties, they are permitted to retire, but are continued indefinitely on the payroll at a reduced figure.

An even more common policy where no formal retirement plan has been established is to permit all employees to continue on in their positions at full salaries beyond customary retirement ages, even though their work grows less and less effective. This policy can prove to be very expensive and may also impair the efficiency of an organization.

Either of the above mentioned policies results in charging current expenses with "human obsolescence" charges that were incurred in previous years and should have been set up as reserves and charged as operating expenses in such years.

The general level of bank salaries does not permit most bank employees to accumulate any sizable amount of reserves out of their earnings to provide for their retirement, nor to supplement to any considerable extent the social security benefits and any other retirement benefits to which they might be entitled. This is true of both officers and employees since those in the higher salary brackets usually have additional civic and social responsibilities which occasion greater living expenses. With present income tax rates and high living costs, it is virtually impossible for any bank employee with a wife and children who takes any active part in the life of the community, to save any substantial amount out of his salary.

The principal reasons why so many banks as well as other employers have adopted employee retirement plans may be summarized as follows:

1. To improve employee morale and decrease employee turnover.

2. To increase personal efficiency of active employees through contentment and lack of worry over the future.

3. To provide an economical and fair method of eliminating inefficient, aged employees.

4. To fulfill a moral obligation for satisfactory, continuous, and faithful service.

5. To meet the financial needs of dependent, superannuated or disabled employees.

6. The encouragement of thrift by employees (in contributory plans).

It is noteworthy that there is a substantial difference between the "cost" of provision for retirement where the company bears the cost (or most of it) on the one hand, and where the employees bear it, on the other hand. Assuming a 52% Federal Income Tax and a 6% State Excise Tax, the cost of each dollar set aside by a bank for retirement purposes is 42 cents. The cost of each such dollar to an employee in the lowest income tax bracket is $1.20, or more than double, since he not only gets no deduction for this purpose, but he must also pay 20 cents out of his other income to pay the tax on the dollar he sets aside. To the employees in the higher salary classes, the difference in cost is even greater. For instance, with a $12,000 income, the "cost" per dollar of saving, is approximately $1.50. Over a period of twenty-five years or more, this additional impediment in compounding income makes a startlingly substantial difference in the net result.

A reasonable ideal at which to aim in establishing a retirement plan is to seek to provide an income of approximately half of an employee's final pay rate when the employee reaches retirement age.

Any retirement plan which does not assure that all officers and employees, after reaching retirement age, can retire with an income of approximately half of the final pay rate, will probably not be entirely satisfactory for the following reasons:

(a) No bank can afford to force retirement of an officer or employee if the retirement benefits plus social security benefits and other income which the beneficiary might have, will not permit him to live approximately in the manner to which he has been accustomed.

(b) If, when any employee reaches retirement age, it is realized that the retirement benefits are inadequate for proper support, the bank will no doubt have to postpone the time of retirement beyond the specified age, and keep the person in question on the payroll.

(c) If the retirement benefits do not assure, with reasonable certainty, a living income, then the employees will not have the contentment and lack of financial worry that is supposed to be one of the principal benefits of a retirement plan.

(d) It may be argued that some benefits at retirement age are better than no benefits at all, but the fact remains that if the benefits are not sufficient to enable the retired person to live comfortably, compulsory retirement will not be practicable and the plan will not operate.

If the retirement benefits outlined above as desirable are to be provided within a period shorter than fifteen to twenty years after establishment of the plan, it will be necessary to fund the past service credits of all eligible employees.

The cost of funding the past service credits of a bank which has been in business a long time may be quite large. Such cost is usually amortized over a period of years. In fact for income tax purposes the cost cannot be amortized in a period of less than ten years.

In most banks the factor that will probably control the decision whether or not to establish a formal retirement plan, and if so, what type of plan, is the *cost*. It is easy enough to prepare an ideal plan if costs do not have to be considered, but any business organization must necessarily choose a retirement plan that its earnings will justify.

Before a bank can estimate the costs of a retirement plan, the details of a plan must be determined and actuarial computations prepared based on the number of eligible employees, their ages, years of service, and rates of pay.

Before choosing a particular plan, it would be prudent to compare the cost of several different plans or combinations of plans and weigh the advantages of the various proposals. In selecting a retirement plan, an employer has two general fields in which to make a choice:

1. A pension plan.

2. A profit-sharing plan, with benefits deferred until retirement.

Each of the two plans has certain advantages and disadvantages. Among the advantages of the pension plan may be listed the following:

1. Such a plan, if funded, (or plans made to fund it over a period) may be made immediately operative.

2. A pension plan actuarially computed provides certain definite benefits which may be calculated and stated in advance.

Among the disadvantages of a pension plan to be considered are:

1. Such a plan places a fixed financial obligation on the employer in bad times as well as good, and abandonment of the plan will undoubtedly hurt employee morale and efficiency.

2. Since the benefits from a pension plan become a fixed obligation of the employer, they are apt to be accepted by employees as a definite part of their compensation, and therefore offer no continued incentive to employees to help increase profits.

3. As pointed out above, the cost of funding the past service benefits in an organization which has a large number of employees with long service, will amount to a considerable sum.

Among the chief advantages of a profit-sharing retirement plan are the following points:

1. The employer's payments are limited to a percentage of profits and the plan cannot, therefore, become an undue financial burden.

2. A profit sharing plan should offer employees a continuing incentive to increase the efficiency of the organization and increase the profits in which they will share.

The principal disadvantage of a profit-sharing retirement plan is that it offers no assurance to either the employee or to the employer that any employee will, upon reaching retirement age, be able to live out of the funds that will be available for him.

A second disadvantage is that such a plan cannot really begin to operate until at least fifteen or twenty years after it is inaugurated, because in the meantime the accumulations for the individual employees will not be sufficient to permit any employee to live out of his retirement benefits.

It appears that an ideal plan would be (1) a pension plan which, with social security benefits, will provide the necessities of life after retirement age, plus (2) a profit-sharing retirement plan which will provide an incentive for increased profits out of which employees can hope to receive retirement pay which will be adequate to provide more than just bare necessities.

After the general type of retirement plan has been determined, that is, a pension plan or a profit sharing plan, or a combination of the two, there are certain other decisions that must be made concerning the specifications of the plan. Some of the features that must be decided upon are:

1. The retirement benefits which the plan is intended to provide. (The retirement benefits that the plan will provide will depend upon the past service benefit formula

and the future service formula that is adopted.)

2. The conditions of eligibility, that is, the minimum and maximum age for participants and the years of service required.

3. The effective retirement age and provisions, if any, for early retirement before attaining the retirement age.

4. The conditions under which the participation of an employee in the retirement fund will become vested, that is to say, whether an eligible employee leaving the bank voluntarily or through discharge for cause will forfeit all rights to participation in the retirement fund.

5. Whether the plan will be contributory or non-contributory, that is, whether the bank will bear the entire cost or whether the employees will contribute to the cost of the plan.

6. Whether the plan will be insured with an insurance company or whether the fund will be invested by a trustee.

7. If the fund is to be invested, a decision must be made as to whether it will be self-administered by the bank as trustee, or whether such investment management will be handled in some other manner.

Each of the seven factors listed above requires careful study. No general rules or recommendations can be made on these questions without full and complete knowledge of all of the facts concerning the bank under consideration.

Since the preparation of a retirement plan should be a tailor-made job, fitting the specific situation of the bank in question, and involving a number of actuarial computations, the preliminary planning and cost estimates should be made by someone with wide experience in this field, and possessing the ability to make the necessary actuarial computations. The cost of such professional service will be small as compared with the potential amounts involved in a retirement plan. There are a number of firms who offer professional services as pension consultants. Most city banks will be in a position to render consultant service to their correspondent banks on this subject, and to recommend the services of a pension consultant or actuary if one is needed.

Banks which have not already done so should give serious study to the desirability of an appropriate employee retirement plan. Even for the very small banks, it is often possible through association "group pension plans" and sometimes through the "group plans" of correspondent banks, to work out satisfactory retirement plans. Each bank will have a somewhat different situation that must be met in the manner most appropriate to that institution, but the decision for a "formal plan" or "no plan" should be made after adequate study and with full information.

In the above discussion, profit sharing plans have been treated as one method of providing retirement benefits. This was based on the assumption that the profit sharing benefits would be delayed until retirement. Such deferment is not essential to a profit sharing plan although it does offer some advantages to both the employer and employee.

Perhaps the simplest form of profit sharing plan and the type that has been most commonly used by banks, is the Christmas bonus paid in cash near the end of the calendar year at the discretion of the Board of Directors.

While this form of profit sharing, or bonus, is undeniably popular with employees, it nevertheless presents some difficulties from the employer's viewpoint.

If there is any direct or implied promise on the part of the employer that such a bonus will be paid, the bonus loses its discretionary character and will be considered by the Wage-Hour Board as a part of the basic wage. In such event the bonus must be included in computing wages for overtime purposes.

The fact that a Christmas bonus has been paid at the same rate for a number of consecutive years, has been held sufficient to remove its "discretionary" status and cause it to be included in the basic wage.

During a continuing period of inflation, employers found it necessary and desirable to increase the rate of the Christmas bonus from time to time, thereby retaining its discretionary status, but such increases cannot realistically be expected to continue indefinitely.

The decision to reduce or forego entirely the payment of a discretionary Christmas bonus that has been well established by precedent is almost certain to result in employee resentment.

The fact that a discretionary bonus cannot be announced or depended upon until it is passed on by the Board of Directors leaves an element of uncertainty that the employees dislike. This uncertainty can also cause some anxiety on the part of the executive officer who will have the unpleasant duty of announcing "No bonus" to the staff.

In paying a cash bonus, it is of course necessary to deduct the appropriate amount of withholding tax for income tax purposes. Such withholding taxes sometimes account for a surprisingly large portion of the aggregate bonus.

A profit sharing plan that is based on a predetermined formula and the benefits distributable at the termination of active employment presents a number of advantages.

1. Since the benefits are based on a formula, and are contingent upon the net profits reaching certain minimum figures, it removes the burden from management and the

Board of deciding whether a bonus shall be declared.

2. The employees' share in the profits will not be dependent upon the whims of management or the Board.

3. Since the distribution of benefits is deferred, no withholding taxes are deducted, and the beneficiaries will get the benefit of compound interest on the gross amount until distribution. Considerable tax advantage may be enjoyed by having the benefits taxed as a capital gain at retirement.

4. The accumulated benefits distributable at retirement or termination of employment will likely serve a more useful purpose than if such benefits had been distributed in annual installments.

5. Retirement will not be dreaded and avoided if sizable benefits have been built up through a profit sharing plan.

6. As previously pointed out under the discussion of profit sharing retirement plans, a profit sharing plan contingent upon satisfactory earnings relieves the employer from a fixed financial obligation which in some years it can ill afford.

As is the case in retirement plans, the designing of a profit sharing plan for a particular bank calls for a number of decisions at the local level concerning such matters as:

1. The formula for determining the employer's contribution to the profit sharing fund.

2. The conditions of eligibility for participating employees.

3. The circumstances and conditions under which employees may make withdrawals from their participating shares prior to retirement or termination of employment.

4. Conditions under which employees' participating shares will be forfeited to the fund.

It would perhaps be ideal from both the employer's and the employees' viewpoint if it were possible to set up a profit sharing formula and permit the individual employees to elect each year whether they will receive the profit sharing benefits in cash or whether they will be deferred until retirement. However, the present federal revenue laws provide that such a right to elect cash distribution makes the distributable benefits taxable in that year whether they are received or not, thereby removing the tax advantage incident to deferment.

A bank adopting either a pension plan or a profit sharing plan should be careful that the plan qualifies with the U. S. Treasury Department as an "exempt plan" for Federal income tax purposes. If the contributions of an employer are to be treated as allowable deductions as business expense for income taxes, the plan must be submitted to the District Director of Internal Revenue and be declared a qualified and exempt plan. The rules that will qualify a plan as tax exempt are fairly simple, but should be well understood by the persons preparing the plan.

Banks which operate trust departments have found that trusteeships of both pension plans and profit sharing plans can be attractive and remunerative if a sufficient volume of such trusts can be obtained in the bank's trade area. Before undertaking the administration of such trusts, the bank should make certain that its staff includes competent personnel to handle this type of trust business.

There is a wealth of material available on both retirement plans and profit sharing plans for those who wish to pursue the matter further. Prentice Hall publishes a looseleaf service which covers all phases of the subject. The council of Profit Sharing Industries, Akron, Ohio, has published a manual which is an authoritative guide in connection with profit sharing plans. Bankers Trust Company, of New York, has from time to time published a study of retirement plans, containing analyses of retirement programs adopted by leading commercial and industrial organizations, including other banks.

CHAPTER V

Salary Administration

ONLY IN RECENT YEARS has the subject of the fair measurement of bank salaries received serious consideration and study. In too many instances, the fixing of salaries has been a haphazard process without any attempt to handle it on an equitable basis. Many employers have never considered adjustments except in response to complaints. Raises have gone to the employees who have been most aggressive in their own behalf, while others, just as valuable, have remained at low levels, or perhaps sought new jobs.

Theoretically, the salary of each employee is a confidential matter, but actually, employees invariably learn what others are earning, and it seems universal that the news of raises in salaries travels fast.

Progressive employers, realizing that dissatisfied employees are seldom efficient, and that salaries are the most frequent cause of employment discontent, have learned that salary administration is one of the most important phases of management.

To most people the salary which they receive is the

47

most important point about their jobs. This is true because salary usually determines the manner in which they must live.

Next to present salary, the most important factor is the opportunity for advancement, but this really means the possibility for salary increases.

Recognition of accomplishments, prestige, titles, working hours, time off, physical environment, and other working conditions make some jobs more attractive than others, but in large measure, salary is the most important job factor with most employed people.

What is a fair and proper manner of determining salaries? To some extent human effort or labor is like any other commodity, and its value is determined by supply and demand. This is known as the commodity concept of labor. If the work to be performed requires a high degree of skill and special training, there will be fewer persons available for such work, and therefore, the pay will be higher. If the work is simple and the position easily filled, the pay will be lower.

The commodity concept of labor by management is now more or less obsolete insofar as salary administration is concerned. Wise management has learned that it is not good business to fix wages and salaries at the lowest levels which will attract sufficient workers to fill all positions.

A sociological change has been taking place in business and industry with reference to wages and salaries in recent years. Partly through pressure from organized labor, and to a large extent as a result of progress in human relations, the worker's share of income as compared to the owner's share has steadily increased. Both higher living standards and the high cost of living have been contributing factors in this gradual change. There has been a further tendency to narrow the gap between the highest paid employees and those in the lower brackets.

These economic and sociological factors have a definite effect on the long-range trend of salaries, but do not directly enter into the current administration of a salary program.

In determining a fair and proper salary for any individual worker, three questions must be asked and answered:

1st: What is the job?
2nd: What is the value of the job to the employer?
3rd: How well does the individual perform the job?

These three questions involve three separate phases of salary administration.

The first is job description.

The second is job evaluation.

The third is merit rating.

Any sound salary administration program will necessarily involve these three steps.

Job Description

Obviously, before a job can be evaluated and a particular person's performance and worth in the job can be determined, there must be a clear understanding by all concerned as to what the job is.

A job description should be prepared for each job in the bank, listing all of the duties required to be performed on each individual job.

In addition to listing the duties, the job description should specify the:

(a) Knowledge requirements.
(b) Skill requirements.
(c) Physical requirements.

(d) Responsibility requirements.

(e) Supervision requirements.

Job Evaluation

After obtaining satisfactory job descriptions on each individual job, the next step is job evaluation, and this is unquestionably the most important part of any salary administration program.

There are many different methods of job evaluation. One is known as "Job Ranking", which means that every job in the company is arranged in order from the least important with the lowest requirements, to the most difficult with the maximum requirements. After the ranking has been accomplished, minimum and maximum rates may be established in accordance with the relationship of each job group. While this is perhaps the simplest method of job evaluation, it is only suitable in relatively small banks.

Another method that is perhaps the most popular means of job evaluation is known as the "Factor Comparison Plan". Under this method, the following characteristics of each job are studied:

1. Preparation required for the job.
   (That is, education or experience requirements necessary for a beginner.)
2. Personal qualifications required.
   (Under this heading, such qualifications as appearance, conversational ability, personality, courtesy, force, vigor, perseverance, tactfulness, rapidity, accuracy, initiative, supervisory ability, and other such personal characteristics are considered.)
3. The complexity of the duties required by the job are appraised. Whether or not the work is routine and requires very little judgment, or whether it is

difficult or involved and requires unusual care and attention as well as independent thinking and judgment; whether or not new problems are faced that frequently require important decisions.

4. Responsibility.
(Whether the job involves the possibility of directly increasing profits or incurring losses for the company.)

5. Human Relations.
(Whether the job necessitates successful contacts with other people; either the public, customers, or fellow employees.)

6. Degree of executive responsibility.
(This factor is concerned with the degree to which the job requires the supervision and control of other people in the bank.)

Under each of these six factors are listed appropriate classifications usually beginning with the simplest requirements, and proceeding progressively to the most difficult requirements. In each instance, there is an appropriate description that may be indicated by a check mark.

This type of rating sheet should be completed at several levels. First, the workers themselves should be allowed to analyze their own jobs and indicate what factors they think are required, and which of the several classifications for each factor best fit the job. It will usually be found that the worker is likely to overrate the job and describe it as more exacting and difficult than supervisors at higher levels, but nevertheless, the worker's viewpoint is important and cannot be entirely ignored.

Three columns are provided on the form, and after the worker has checked the appropriate factors in the first column, it is submitted to the immediate supervisor or department head for a second rating. When a large number of workers hold the same job title, the average, or composite rating by the workers should be considered by the supervisor in his evaluation. After the supervisor has made his evaluation, the rating sheet should go to a central committee at the administrative or executive level, who will determine the final evaluation, taking into consideration the evaluations made by the workers and the supervisor.

A further refinement of the factor comparison plan which carries it a step further, is known as the "Point Rating Plan." This method involves the assignment of point values to each of the factors on the job evaluation sheet, and then subdivides these points to the extent that the highest point value will carry the maximum value for the factor. Thus, if maximum experience, for example, is rated at ten points, jobs requiring the least experience will be assigned one point, and jobs requiring no previous experience will be assigned a zero rating for this factor.

This point assignment is also applied to all other job factors and the number of points assigned to any factor may be weighted in accordance with the belief of the management as to the importance of that factor on a particular job.

Where the point rating plan is used, the point values of the various factors are ordinarily not known to those below the top management level, so that evaluations will not be unduly influenced by the numerical score. A specimen of a job evaluation point summary sheet is shown as an exhibit.

In some cases there have been attempts to relate evaluation points to dollars of salary, but such a system presents a number of difficulties which make such evaluations, to a large extent, synthetic or artificial.

After the relative difficulty of the various jobs in the

organization has been determined through job evaluation sheets as described above, it is desirable to determine an appropriate minimum and maximum rate for each job classification.

In each group the minimum rate is intended for a beginner who is believed to have the ultimate qualifications for the position, but who will require additional training and experience before performing the position in a fully satisfactory manner. The maximum rate is intended to represent the most that can be paid for the position when it is performed by a fully trained, competent and experienced employee in the most efficient manner possible.

In jobs involving interstate commerce, which include all banking positions, the Wage-Hour laws have established minimum hourly rates of pay. Therefore it is mandatory to hire people at rates not lower than the minimum rate specified by law.

In fixing a minimum and maximum rate for each wage group, the employer cannot depend entirely upon his own valuation estimate based on the productive value to the employer, but the employer must realize that he is in competition with other employers for high caliber personnel and salary rates must be comparable to what other employers are paying for similar work. Any job evaluation program must, therefore, include research into prevailing rates for similar work in that locality.

It is also timely to note at this point that a job evaluation is not a one-time task, but must be reviewed periodically for needed adjustments caused by changes in prevailing wage rates, the cost of living, labor shortages, and other such economic factors.

In evaluating a particular job, care must be exercised not to appraise the individual who is currently holding that

JOB EVALUATION POINT SUMMARY

JOB TITLE............................ DEPT............................ DATE...............

FACTORS	RATING	FACTORS	RATING
TRAINING AND EXPERIENCE		**B. RESPONSIBILITY**	
A. 1. Education	....	15. Monetary	....
2. Special Knowledge	....	16. Material	....
B. 1. Minimum		17. Equipment and Other Property	....
Experience	....	18. Internal Goodwill	....
C. 1. New factors to be		19. External Goodwill	....
learned	....	20. Records, Reports, Facts	....
D. 1. Physical		21. Confidential Information	....
requirements	....	22. Business Development	....
2. Basic skills		23. Methods, Processes and Procedures	....
needed	....	24. Work of others	....
		25. Health & Safety of Others	....
SKILL & SPECIAL APPTITUDES			
1. Executive ability	....	**C. PHYSICAL REQUIREMENTS**	
2. Supervision	....		
3. Creative ability	....	26. Mental Alertness	....
4. Independency of Action	....	27. Monotony	....
5. Analytical Ability	....	28. Strenuousness	....
6. Judgment	....	29. Disagreeableness	....
7. Complexity of Duties	....		
8. Written Expression	....	**D. SPECIAL INFORMATION**	
9. Oral Expression	....	1. Frequency of Supervision	....
10. Cooperativeness	....		
11. Personal Appearance	....	**TOTAL EVALUATED RATING**	....
12. Manner (Personality)	....	Present Wage Range ....to..........	
13. Tact	....	Evaluated Wage Range ....to..........	
14. Dexterity	....	Evaluated by .... Checked by	

54

EMPLOYEE PROGRESS REPORT

NAME _____DEPARTMENT _____

REPORT FOR PERIOD ENDED _____

IMPORTANT — Please fill out each item as completely as possible, as the basis for a helpful discussion with the employee.

. HOW WELL DOES THE EMPLOYEE KNOW HIS JOB? _____

_____

_____

_____

He Could IMPROVE His Job Knowledge By _____

_____

. HOW WELL DOES THE EMPLOYEE PERFORM HIS WORK, BOTH AS TO

QUALITY AND AMOUNT? _____

_____

_____

He Could IMPROVE His Job Performance By _____

_____

_____

55

3. IS THERE ANYTHING EXCEPTIONALLY GOOD OR POOR ABOUT THE EM-
PLOYEE'S PERSONAL QUALITIES? (Consider such traits as Receptiveness to Suggestions, Willingness to Help Others, Ability to Get along with Fellow Employees, Attendance
and Tardiness Record, Personal Appearance, Ability to Meet the Public, and Loyalty to
the Bank. If you think the employee is misplaced in his present job, also indicate that.)

_____

_____

_____

He Could IMPROVE His Personal Qualities By _____

_____

REMARKS: _____

_____

RECORD OF INTERVIEW

This report was discussed with the employee on _____. His reaction
                                                          Date

to my suggestion for improvement was _____

_____

The employee appears to be (check which) Well Satisfied _____ Satisfied _____

Dissatisfied _____ with his job.

The discussion also revealed that _____

_____

Signed: _____

job. The requirements of the job itself are being appraised rather than a particluar person.

Generally speaking, the greater the education, experience, and skill required for any position, the harder it will be to fill it satisfactorily and, therefore, the higher will be the salary.

Job requirements which carry great weight in determining the amount of compensation to allocate to a particular job are:

1. Leadership, or capacity to supervise the work of others.
2. Judgment, or the capacity to make wise decisions.
3. The ability to serve customers tactfully and inspire confidence.
4. The ability to work without supervision.

The allocation of price tags or salary brackets to each group of jobs can only be accomplished after considering all of the matters discussed above. In most cases, it will require a long period of trial and error and frequent adjustments before the relative rates can be satisfactorily determined. As a matter of fact, it is a job that is never finished.

Merit Rating

Once salary brackets are established for each job group, the final step is to fix the appropriate rate within his respective bracket for each individual employee.

This phase of salary management is usually called merit rating. It is ordinarily accomplished by department heads filling out a rating form, classifying each employee as to the manner in which he or she performs the various aspects of the job.

Instead of a rating form with point valuations indicating the degree of excellence for various job factors, which is used as an advisory report to management, some banks have adopted a program of rating known as "Employee Progress Reporting." A specimen of such a report form is shown as an exhibit.

Under such a plan, each employee's Progress Report is made out by his department head. If there is a sub-department head who directly supervises the employee, he is consulted and collaborates in making out the report. After the department head has filled out the form in consultation with the immediate supervisor, if any, an interview with the employee is planned. This system of interviews with employees provides, in effect, a continuous bank-wide training program, with supervisors at each level assuming the responsibility for the development of the employees who report to them.

To guide the supervisors in preparing Progress Reports and to encourage some degree of uniformity in procedure, one bank has issued the following instructions to supervisors in connection with interviewing employees and preparing Progress Reports:

DISCUSSING PROGRESS REPORTS WITH EMPLOYEES

"After the department head has filled out the form in consultation with the immediate supervisor, if any, the interview with the employee is planned. If the officer feels that the employee may, during the interview, inquire about his current prospects for promotion or salary increase, he should be prepared to answer such questions honestly and completely. Getting the answers in advance is a part of good interview planning. The giving of answers to such questions as they arise in the interview avoids any suggestion of 'buck passing' and increases the officer's prestige as a part of management.

"Since it is important that this interview be handled as skillfully as possible, several practical suggestions follow:

STUDY THE EMPLOYEE

"Check through on his performance, review his attendance record, and make sure to have all the facts. Never mention a weakness to an employee unless you are dead sure you have the facts to substantiate it.

"List the employee's strong points and his weak ones — where he has done good work and where he has slipped up. It is just as important to praise him as it is to point out his weaknesses.

"Use this as a guide in planning the contact, then, when you are clear in your own mind the points where he should improve, try to be constructive. Never point out a fault unless you can suggest some way in which it can be corrected.

PLAN THE INTERVIEW

"Decide exactly how you will start, and how you will go from one point to another. Try to work it out so that the employee will feel free to talk, and plan your talk around the improvement program.

CHOOSE THE TIME AND PLACE

"Decide on the best time and place to contact the employee; get someone to take over his job, if necessary, so it won't be on his mind. Conduct the interview at a place where you won't be disturbed.

BE FRIENDLY

"Talk sincerely, in a friendly, helpful manner.

Remember, you may be reprimanding, but you are trying to help the employee to improve.

"Avoid arguments—try to be a good listener.

"Encourage the employee to discuss his problems and try to make the person *want* to improve.

FURTHER SUGGESTIONS

"1. Don't over-emphasize the Form!

"The report form should be in front of the supervisor, and he may want to glance at it from time to time to make sure he is covering all the items. However, reading it to the employee should be avoided. Reading it to the employee may make him feel that he is on trial, and that you are the judge handing down a sentence.

"Put the items on the form in your own words. Keep the interview friendly, natural, and informal. The important thing is your *conversation* with the employee. Keep it conversational.

"2. Encourage the employee to express his reaction:

"As you cover each main point, invite the employee to give you his slant on it. (Some supervisors have found that it even pays to ask the employee for his slant first.) Don't say, 'Do you agree?' Ask: 'How do you feel about that, Jane?'

"Often it is a good idea to let the employee offer some plan for improvement, rather than giving him your ideas. Being human, he will be more likely to carry out the things *he* thinks up, and this is a way of helping to keep his self-respect intact.

"Should you decide to revise any of the statements which you have on the form because of what the employee says, do so in his presence.

"3. Summarize:

"After all the points have been discussed, best results can be obtained by summarizing the strong points and the weak points. This will enable the employee to carry away in 1-2-3 order, the main things which you and he have worked out for him to try to improve on."

Progress reporting is good supervision and good supervision is necessary to make such a plan successful. If employees look forward to their interviews, it is a tribute to the leadership of their supervisors. It also indicates sound management policy that, in addition to friendly, constructive, day-to-day supervision, employees are entitled to periodic summaries of how they are getting along and what they can do to improve.

Every employee, not only likes to know, but has the right to know, how he is getting along on his job. An employee cannot be expected to measure up to his supervisor's expectations unless he knows what these expectations are, nor to improve himself unless he knows just where improvement is needed.

One of a supervisor's fundamental duties, therefore, is to supply this information to each of his employees— clearly, honestly, and in such a way that it will be helpful. This is done most effectively by a combination of two methods:

(1) Day-to-day constructive criticism and praise, as the circumstances warrant, and

(2) Periodic overall summaries of actual job performance as compared to supervisory expectations.

This kind of supervisory leadership which progress reporting represents is mutually advantageous. The supervisor's job is made easier if his employees are constantly trying to improve. By taking sufficient added interest in each employee to review his work with him regularly, the supervisor gets to know each employee better. Employee reactions which are not normally obtained in the course of day-to-day job relations, frequently arise in the course of a well-conducted progress interview. The result is improved understanding and better cooperation on the job.

In the author's bank, all employees were formerly reviewed four times a year, which meant that the salary committee reviewed one-third of the employees each month. In order to give a more careful review to each individual, the reviews were reduced from four times a year to twice a year. The salary reviewing committee meets monthly, but reviews only one-sixth of the employees each month, instead of one-third.

The fact that department heads are required to review all employees twice a year and rate the manner of their job performance insures all employees that they cannot be forgotten, and that their salary situation will be reviewed by the immediate department head, as well as senior management, at least twice a year. Under such a plan, it should never be necessary for an employee to initiate a request for a salary increase. Whether he gets a desired increase or not, at least he knows that his situation was considered and discussed.

This plan of job description, job evaluation, and merit rating is practicable and workable and with some variations it is being used in a large number of banks. There is no panacea in salary administration that will please everyone. Practically no one is able to make an accurate estimate of his or her value to the employer. All of us are inclined to be conscious of our good points and remain blissfully blind to our shortcomings. As long as human nature retains its age-old characteristics and Americans are possessed of their traditional ambition to get ahead, we will have employees who are discontented with their salaries.

It must be recognized that often people are capable of being promoted faster than promotional opportunities are presented. Generally speaking, people cannot be paid more and more indefinitely for continuing to do the same work. Theoretically at least, salary increases come only as employees, through increased production or increased responsibilities, become more valuable to the employer.

There are many mistaken ideas about salaries that have gained widespread acceptance. One of these is that the longer a person works on a given job, the more salary he should receive. This is true to a very limited extent. A beginner on a job naturally receives a lower salary while he is learning and should expect reasonable increases as he gains experience and efficiency. After the job is thoroughly learned, however, and the employee no longer increases his output or efficiency, there is no basis for expecting the salary to continue to increase.

Once an employee has mastered a particular job and cannot reasonably expect to increase its productive value, then, if he is ambitious, he should look ahead to another job with increased responsibilities and a higher salary.

In recent years, the rise in the cost of living has caused much discussion of the relationship between wages and the cost of living. It is interesting to note that rising living costs are used as a lever to increase wage rates, though labor unions resist the efforts of management to have this work in reverse by tying wages to the cost of living index.

The cost of living index, nevertheless, is a factor to be considered in the overall job evaluation process rather than in determining an appropriate salary for a particular individual. Fluctuations in the cost of living constitute one among several reasons why any evaluation of jobs must be reviewed and readjusted from time to time.

In valuing jobs in any organization, the rates paid for similar jobs in other business institutions in the vicinity are a significant factor, but should not necessarily be the final, determining reason. If wage rates are established at a higher level than prevails in the industry, it will be difficult to compete with competitors whose costs are lower. Good management should attempt to establish salary rates above those of similar concerns, and yet, through efficient operations, keep total operating expenses at a satisfactory level.

Higher wage rates might be expected to increase operating efficiency, but unfortunately, this is not always true. On the other hand, substandard wage rates nearly always result in mediocre performance. Not only are underpaid employees low in morale, and indifferent to their work, but low wage rates over a sustained period of years have a tendency to cause ambitious, better class employees to seek better pay elsewhere, leaving the organization with mediocre personnel.

The problem of salary administration has been vastly complicated by the federal legislation in this field. Not only do we have to reckon with what we think is just and equitable to pay our employees, but we have to adjust our salary administration to a whole maze of bureaucratic regulations which are constantly changing.

Most of these observations about salaries would be applicable to almost any type of business. However, there are some aspects of salary administration which are peculiar to banks. In the past, bank salaries have been proverbially low in comparison with the pay for similar work and responsibilities in other lines of business and industry. This is stated as a fact, without attempting to justify or defend it.

There are a number of reasons why bank salaries have been proverbially low. One of these is because banks in the past have been able to offer working conditions that were more attractive than in many other business establishments. These factors have included attractive, comfortable working quarters, convenient location, association with high type people, relatively short hours, and frequent holidays. As a result of a reputation for good working conditions, banks in the past have usually had no difficulty in getting plenty of employment applications. In recent years, however, other lines of business have made more progress than banking in improving working conditions. The widespread prevalence of the five-day week, air-conditioned working quarters, and higher rates of pay in other lines of business, have resulted in fewer applications for bank employment. This is particularly true for positions above the clerical level.

Banks have attained an unfavorable reputation for low pay and slow advancement among college students and surveys among college seniors show that banking is near the bottom as a choice of vocations in that group.

One of the reasons that banking has a reputation for low pay is that banking operations require a large volume of routine clerical transactions that must be performed at low cost. No matter how long a worker remains on one of these routine clerical jobs, there is a rather low ceiling limit on possible salary. Therefore, steady increases in salary must require graduation from routine clerical work into higher responsibilities involving possibilities of increasing profits or avoiding losses, or supervision of the work of others.

As pointed out above, people unfortunately are often capable of being advanced faster than opportunities are presented. After all, in every bank there are a limited number of executive positions, and there are sometimes more people capable of holding good jobs than there are good jobs available.

On the other hand, it is often true that when one of the top jobs in a bank is open, the position requires special qualifications that are not possessed by anyone in the organization. This is an unhappy situation, but when it arises, management has no alternative but to seek someone on the outside who has the necessary specialized qualifications. The only way to avoid this situation is long range planning through training courses and other such means to plan for a suitable replacement for each position in the bank, especially the key positions. Since it is not always practicable to have people two deep in every position, particularly where highly trained specialists are required, it is difficult to always have an available replacement ready.

One controversy with reference to bank salaries that will probably never be settled is the relative importance of the several functions in the bank. The various functions of banking are similar to the positions on a baseball team or football team. All of the positions must be satisfactorily filled if the team performs well and any weak position can ruin a good team.

Traditionally in banks, the banking operations jobs have not usually paid as much as comparable positions in lending, investments, and trusts. It's more or less like the backfield on a football team getting the credit for making touchdowns, but the players in the line are often the unsung heroes.

The Federal Reserve banks each year compile and

publish the average operating ratios of member banks. One of the ratios included is the percentage of salaries and wages to total earnings. It is noteworthy to observe that salaries and wages are the largest item of expense for banks.

The ratios published by the Federal Reserve Bank enable any bank to determine whether its total expenditures for salaries are in line with those of other banks.

In the Sixth Federal Reserve District this ratio was 29.2 for all member banks in 1961. The high during the ten-year period from 1952 through 1961 was 32.3 in 1954 and the low was 28.3 in 1960. The fact that this important ratio has declined during this ten-year period does not mean that bank salaries have tended to decrease, because it is certain that the trend for individual salaries has been upward; the decreased ratio results from the fact that during this decade banks have enjoyed a substantial increase in earnings.

In conclusion, almost any sort of salary administration plan is better than no plan. But a successful plan will depend almost entirely upon the quality of its administration. No matter how good the plan, unless it has the unqualified support of top management, it doesn't have much chance of success.

Finally, any formalized plan of salary administration must be tempered with human understanding and common sense.

CHAPTER VI

The Bank Building

As PREVIOUSLY INDICATED, the people who compose the bank staff, their abilities and attitude, are the most important factor in determining the caliber of a particular bank. Second in importance, perhaps, are the policies and procedures followed in rendering banking service. Perhaps third in importance are the physical facilities of the bank which will include buildings and equipment.

Location is of some importance though perhaps is not emphasized as much as in some other types of business. Where branch banking is authorized, strategically located branches make it possible to literally take banking facilities to the customer's neighborhood.

The automobile and traffic congestion are causing new trends and a new pattern in bank buildings as well as in nearly all other lines of business.

A major decision of management in connection with a bank building is whether to own or rent. In the past, it has been traditionally popular for the larger and medium sized banks to own their banking premises. Under some circumstances, however, it may be more expedient to rent. A newly organized bank which has not had time to build up its capital structure may not find it feasible to invest its own capital in a building. If there is a sizable mortgage debt on the bank building, the bank may not want to have the mortgage liability in its statement, and may utilize a subsidiary building corporation for this purpose.

Under some circumstances, there may be a tax advantage in paying rent on a building rather than owning, indeed some banks have utilized sales and lease back agreements for this purpose.

In any event, the building expense, whether it be in the form of employed capital or rental, should be in proper proportion to the bank's assets and earnings.

Another decision of importance in connection with the bank building is whether it shall be exclusively for the bank's own use, or whether some portion of it shall be designed for use by other tenants. Partly for prestige purposes, many banks erect so-called "sky-scraper" buildings with the expectation of leasing a majority of the space to others.

A building of this type also offers possibility of expansion of the banking space if the need arises. It is not economically expedient to invest money in portions of a building not needed for banking purposes, unless the net rental return after all expenses, plus depreciation and obsolescence, is commensurate with the return that the bank might reasonably expect if the invested capital was employed in its banking business.

To obtain maximum rental returns some banks lease the ground floor space to stores and locate the banking rooms on the mezzanine, or upper floors. Ground floor locations for banking rooms are usually considered necessary in smaller towns and cities, but in the larger cities, upper floor locations have been found satisfactory.

Any bank that is at all optimistic about its future growth should keep expansion in mind in planning its building.

As suggested above, the automobile has caused a revolution in bank design and architecture. Nearby parking facilities, preferably adjoining the bank, are considered of prime importance in any new bank building, whether it be in a suburb or downtown area. Drive-in tellers windows are also considered a "must" if they can possibly be provided.

Bank design, like many other fields of architecture, has been radically changed in recent years. A generation ago, it was considered necessary to install massive steel bars at all windows and give banks the appearance of a penitentiary as a suggestion of strength and invulnerability. Actually, so long as a bank has a substantial vault, there is no reason why its doors and windows should be barred against burglars. The modern trend in banks is to plate glass fronts that invite entrance rather than to suggest the repelling of intruders. The use of marble and ornate decoration has given way to less formal treatment. Tellers' "cages" are being supplanted by counter type tellers' installations.

Many banks in the past have believed that it was desirable to have all of the officers on a "platform" adjacent to the main lobby where they were visible to all customers and readily accessible to all comers. This may be desirable for officers who open accounts or approve checks and other such operating items, but for lending officers, trust officers, and executive officers who handle confidential matters for customers privacy is important. This privacy is not for the officers' benefit, but is greatly desired by customers. Research in this direction reveals that many customers are embarrassed by discussing loans or other such matters at an officer's desk in full view of all passers-by in the lobby. The factor of reasonable privacy appears more important than accessibility for this type of business.

Bank credit officers know that poor housekeeping in a customer's store, office or plant, is sometimes an indication of slipshod methods in other areas of operation. Banks should, therefore, be careful that their banking rooms and offices at all times will present a neat and orderly appearance. It is surprising that some banks that are otherwise well run, are careless in their housekeeping. In every bank, some responsible person should be designated to accept responsibility that the banking quarters are kept clean, neat, and attractive. In the larger banks that are departmentalized, some one in each department should supervise the "housekeeping" responsibility, but even though the responsibility is decentralized, some one should oversee the entire bank in this respect.

The physical aspects of branch banking, such as desirable locations, type of building, drive-in equipment, etc., require careful study for each individual situation, and very few rules or suggestions can be made that will be applicable to all cases. The trend in all lines of business seems to be toward decentralization of locations. This is particularly true of service institutions such as banks. Where the laws and local circumstances permit it, banks should give constant study to the possibilities of expansion through additional branches.

CHAPTER VII

Lending Policies and Procedures

THE LENDING OF MONEY is one of the essential functions of a bank. A financial institution that does not lend money is not a bank in the true sense of the word.

The lending function is, therefore, regarded as the essence of banking, and all progressive banks seek earnings through interest on sound loans.

Every bank has loan policies regardless of whether those policies are clearly enunciated and understood by either the lender or the borrower. Often these policies are simply habits and customs that have prevailed over a period of years without anyone taking cognizance that such customs have become established policies. Sometimes the policies are vague and indefinite and are not clearly understood by either the bank staff or its customers. This is easily possible in a bank with a number of different officers engaged in lending, and unless the loan policies are clearly and definitely stated it is more than likely that no two lending officers will follow the same policies.

In a very small bank where the lending is confined to

73

one or two individuals and each is fully familiar with all of the transactions that occur, it may not be necessary to have written loan policies, but in a bank with five or more lending officers it is highly desirable that the lending policies be reduced to writing.

Such policies are, of course, matters for the board of directors to determine, since the responsibility for the bank's loan policies rests squarely upon the board of directors. It would be interesting to ask a half dozen directors of any given bank to describe its loan policies. Unless such policies have been definitely adopted and placed in written form, it is safe to say that each of the six directors would have somewhat different ideas about the policies. The same might even be true among the different officers of a bank.

Since all banks have loan policies, written or not, there seems to be no very plausible argument against reducing the policies to writing. It appears that a bank has everything to gain, and nothing to lose, by clearly establishing its objective with reference to loans through appropriate resolutions of the board of directors.

Assuming that a bank decides it is desirable to adopt loan policies and to make a record of them, what are some of the factors to be considered, and how should the policies be stated? It must be recognized in the beginning that policies governing any phase of a bank's operations must necessarily be limited to broad principles that are flexible enough to cover all contingencies. Neither lending nor any other function that involves the use of discretion and the human equation can be resolved into an exact formula or be governed by a rigid code. Nevertheless, there are certain principles that will be followed in any event, and these principles may be stated in such manner as to leave

74

ample room for freedom of action within appropriate limits.

Among the subjects that might be included in a resolution by a bank's board of directors establishing loan policies, are the following:

1. The general fields of lending in which the bank will engage.

2. Types of loans that the bank will not approve.

3. Rates of interest for various types of loans. (Such rates must be adjusted from time to time to meet changing conditions, and must be flexible enough to cover all situations that may arise.)

4. Maximum limits which the various officers may lend without specific approval.

5. Types of loans and lines of credit that must be approved by the board of directors' loan committee.

6. The trade area in which the bank will seek loans.

(A suggested resolution for a hypothetical, medium sized bank, outlining its lending policies, is set forth in Appendix "A.")

The functions of a bank credit department are essentially the same, regardless of whether the bank is small, medium, or large. It is the business of a bank credit department to gather, classify, analyze, and interpret information concerning borrowers and prospective borrowers. In the very small bank, the credit function will likely be performed by lending officers. In the medium sized bank there is usually a separate credit department which will gather, classify, and analyze the credit information, but the interpretation and credit decision is usually left to the lending officers. In the large bank, the credit department is a large organization in itself, with specialists in each of the various fields of credit.

A medium sized bank with from five to ten lending

officers usually has a separate credit department, employing from four to eight persons. Frequently a lending officer is the head of the credit department, but many banks of this size recognize the importance of a credit department by assigning a full-time, experienced officer to the credit function. Other banks, which apparently do not attach as much importance to the credit department, follow the practice of using a junior officer, or a person who is being trained to become a junior lending officer, as the head of the credit department. It is to be noted that the type of lending in which a bank engages, as well as the volume of loans, will determine its needs with reference to a credit department.

For instance, a bank which attempts to restrict its loans to secured "risk-proof" lending does not have the need for credit facilities that are required in a bank which aggressively seeks business loans. It is the author's belief that in a bank with more than a million dollars of business loans, the credit department should be important enough to justify the use of an experienced officer as the full-time department head.

A fully organized credit department in a medium sized bank will usually require a minimum of four people:—the department head, a statistician or analysis clerk, an investigator, and a stenographer-file clerk. This organization can be expanded to include additional analysts, clerks, investigators, and stenographers, as the situation warrants.

Too often a credit department is merely an organization for filing such credit information as the bank receives, and the department exercises no initiative in seeking and developing information nor in analyzing, interpreting, and using such information as may be available.

Some banks with a small volume of loans are waiting until they obtain a large volume of loans before organizing a credit department. The constructive approach is to organize an adequate credit department in order that the bank may intelligently acquire more good loans. There is a difference of opinion among bankers as to whether it is worth while to build up and maintain credit files on non-customers or non-borrowers. Most aggressive banks build up credit files on non-borrowers and, when a good credit risk is discovered, active steps are taken to encourage loan applications from such sources.

It has been aptly said that anybody can pass on A-1 credit risks, but it takes a real banker to select the good loans from the marginal risks. A well organized credit department can and should supply information of a character that will at least enable lending officers to make "an intelligent guess" in reaching decisions on doubtful loans.

There is no scarcity of literature on the methods of gathering, filing, analyzing, and interpreting credit information, and it is not the purpose of this text to include a discussion of the routine operation of a credit department, nor the analysis of financial statements.

As suggested above, the head of the credit department should be an experienced person, well grounded in credit principles. He should rank along with the lending officers rather than as an apprentice who is training to be a lending officer. As a matter of fact, actual lending experience is a desirable part of the training for a good credit manager. The selection of the department head is, perhaps, the most important step in organizing a successful bank credit department. An aggressive attitude and the ability to analyze and interpret figures are essential qualities for a person in such a position.

Credit departments may be classified into three distinct types, according to the functions they perform and the responsibilities they assume:

1. Those which are purely fact-finding and filing organizations, and play no important part in the credit policies or credit decisions of the bank.

2. Those which determine the extent and character of the investigation and analysis of each case, and which develop and analyze the data assembled, and make a definite recommendation regarding the risk.

3. Those which assume all the responsibilities of the preceding paragraph, and, in addition, actually assume the responsibility of approving or disapproving the loan.*

Credit departments in smaller banks are apt to fit the classification of the paragraph numbered "one" above, while in medium sized banks and larger banks the functions of the credit department correspond to the second paragraph. Rarely does the credit department have the responsibility described in the third paragraph.

The qualifications for a good lending officer in a commercial bank are many. It perhaps is rare that any one man possesses all of the desirable traits and requirements. Although no such person probably exists in the flesh, let us consider the characteristics of an ideal loan officer.

There are certain fields of knowledge that a loan officer must possess if he can be expected to make wise credit decisions. Some lending officers may have acquired a certain amount of this knowledge through the processes of formal education, while others will have had but little formal education, but will have acquired equally as much knowledge through personal study and observation. The lending officer's store of knowledge must include:—a general understanding of the fundamentals of economics in-

---

*Norman H. Morpey, "The Mechanics of the Bank Loan Function," Robert Morris Associates BULLETIN, July 1935.

cluding the principles of production, distribution, and merchandising; a practical knowledge of accounting with the ability to analyze financial statements; thorough familiarity with the principles of commercial law, particularly the law of negotiable instruments, and the customs, usages, and terminology of any lines of business to which the lending officer expects to extend credit.

It is to be noted that comparatively few of the knowledge qualifications can be acquired in a bank except in the credit department or the loan department itself. Unfortunately, long years in the proof department, bookkeeping department, or as a teller, are not particularly helpful in acquiring the type of knowledge that is needed by a lending officer. However, credit investigation, preparing credit files, compiling comparative statements, and computing significant ratios, and other work of this kind in the credit department, are splendid training for a lending officer.

The credit department, therefore, seems to be the best training ground for lending and, in the larger banks with well-organized credit departments, service in this department is nearly always a requisite for a position of making loans.

In the smaller banks where the credit department is largely a place for storing the credit information, and the credit analysis work is performed by the lending officers, there is not much opportunity to gain experience for the lending function. Unfortunately, in many medium sized institutions, there are no facilities for training lending officers and they frequently have to learn through the expensive method of trial and error.

In addition to the knowledge qualifications, there are a number of personal qualifications that a good lending officer should possess. Of course, honesty is a requisite for any bank officer, as well as a high degree of intelligence.

A lending officer of a commercial bank is both a purchasing agent and a salesman. When a borrower applies for a loan, in effect he is trying to sell the loan to the lending officer. On the other hand, a lending officer must constantly be trying to sell the services of the bank to its customers.

As a purchasing agent, the lending officer must be sure that the loan he is considering is of acceptable quality and that the price (the interest rate) is reasonable, and that the term of the loan is appropriate. A good lending officer should seek out and develop good loans, just as a purchasing agent for any other enterprise must seek out and buy commodities, making sure that the terms of the transaction are reasonable.

A good lending officer should not be judged by the small number of his charge-offs, but by the volume of interest earned on the loans he has handled after deducting the charge-offs.

It does not take a skillful loan officer to accept the obviously good loans nor to decline the obviously bad or weak applications. One test of a good loan officer is his ability to guess right most of the time on the borderline applications.

Banks which always say "no" on the borderline cases may avoid chargeoffs and workouts, but, through such riskless lending policies, they are also passing up a lot of good loans.

A good lending officer must have an abiding desire to make loans. Too often we see bank officers who are always looking for some reason why the loan cannot be made instead of trying to work out some type of plan whereby the risk can be minimized and the loan consummated.

The desire to make loans and the self-confidence to make positive decisions are prime requisites in the lending field.

An efficient lending officer is more than just an umpire who says "yes" or "no" to the customer's loan application. A loan officer should strive to be a financial counselor to the borrower. If the loan cannot be made in the manner in which it is presented, perhaps there is some other manner in which it can be handled that will be entirely satisfactory to both parties. If a loan is economically unsound for the borrower, the loan officer should try to show this to him and discourage the loan even though it may be thoroughly safe from the lender's viewpoint.

It is unquestionably true that many good loans are declined because the banker does not have sufficient knowledge of the business in which the borrower is engaged to measure accurately the degree of risk. Since the nature of the risk is not fully understood, the application should properly be declined. However, if the banker knew more about the particular industry or line of business, he could more accurately judge the risk and a larger volume of accepted loans would surely result.

The number of lending officers, and the diversity of the different types of credit extended, will determine to what extent the officers should specialize in certain types of loans. It is certainly more desirable to have a group of "specialists" in a number of credit fields than a group of "jacks-of-all-trades."

In addition to the knowledge qualifications and the personal qualifications of a lending officer, there is one other faculty that he must possess if he is to be reasonably successful in lending. The attribute is the gift of plain common sense. He must be able to size up a situation and determine whether:

1. Borrower seems honest.
2. Borrower's proposal seems reasonable.
3. Figures in the borrower's statement "make sense".
4. Borrower can accomplish the purpose for which the loan is obtained.
5. Borrower has the necessary resources and the "know-how".
6. Purpose of the loan is legitimate.
7. Borrower can probably repay according to schedule.
8. There is a margin of safety if things do not go just right.*

The ability to apply these questions to a pending loan application and to produce the right answers most of the time is the real test of a lending officer.

Since it is one of the functions of the board of directors to approve all loans made by the bank, it is customary for this function to be performed by a directors' committee, but a full report of the committee's actions should be rendered to the board, as the board is charged with responsibility for the committee's actions.

There are two conflicting philosophies concerning the activities of non-officer directors with respect to loans. One school of thought follows the theory that the directors should take an active part in the loan decisions while the opposing philosophy follows the theory that the directors should concern themselves with broad matters of policy only and all credit decisions within those policies should be made by active officers employed for that purpose. The

---

*Notes taken by the author on Lectures in Commercial Banking V, The Graduate School of Banking, New Brunswick, N.J., 1946.

author is of the opinion that the last-mentioned theory is the more sound since by training and experience the lending officers should be more capable of making loan decisions than a non-officer director who devotes only a small portion of his time to such matters.

Non-officer directors, nevertheless, may be of considerable help in a bank's lending program. A director who is familiar with the peculiarities of a particular business or industry should be willing to give the bank the benefit of his specialized information in that field. Directors should also be available for such other credit information as they might possess. One of the advantages of an active directors' loan committee is to interest the directors in the development of new lines of credit. A group of directors who are "loan conscious" can direct many loan applications to a bank which would otherwise never be received.

Practices differ among banks on the desirability of taking written applications on loans. Strangely enough, it is more common to require written applications on small personal loans than on larger loans for business purposes. One reason for this paradox is that the typical application for a small personal loan includes a statement of the borrower's assets and liabilities, and is the only financial statement available, while on larger loans the applicant usually is required to submit a duly authenticated financial statement. It is possible to follow a standardized application form on personal loans, but on business loans it is hard to devise a form that is flexible enough to cover all types of applications.

Since the information concerning real estate mortgage loans is fairly well standardized, it seems to be the practice nearly everywhere to take written applications for all real estate loans.

Although it is impracticable to have a loan application form which is suitable for all types of loans, nevertheless, it is desirable in most cases to have the borrower verify the representations upon which he seeks credit. In some instances this may be done by asking the borrower to write a letter outlining his credit requirements and the facts upon which he bases his request. In many cases it will be inadvisable to require the customer to write such a letter and the lending officer may prefer to dictate a statement for the credit file outlining the circumstances surrounding the loan and ask the customer to verify the accuracy of the credit memorandum by signing it with the lending officer.

Some customers are inclined to be glib and to exaggerate when making oral statements, but are more careful and conservative when stating facts over their signature. This is a strong argument for written loan applications. It does not seem practicable to require a written application on all loans, but it is well to adopt the principle that the borrower's representations upon which a loan is based will be reduced to writing by either the borrower or the lending officer and, wherever practicable, the borrower will be asked to verify the accuracy of such information by his signature.

After the borrower has stated his case and made his application, whether oral or written, the next procedure is the verification of his representations. Of course, the extent of the investigation will depend upon the bank's previous credit experience with the borrower and the circumstances surrounding the proposed loan.

In some rare cases it may not be necessary to investigate and verify the applicant's representations, but the standard procedure should be to verify all essential facts upon which credit is to be based. In most medium sized banks such verifications can be referred to the credit department, which will have trained investigators who will readily know the customary channels and sources for checking credit information.

Where loans are predicated upon financial statements, the lending officer will usually refer the statements to the credit department for tabulation on spread sheets, for comparison with common-sized statements in the same line of business and for the preparation of significant ratio figures. If the bank has had no lending experience in the line of business in which the borrower is engaged, the lending officer will doubtless want the credit department to obtain data on the industry as well as the borrower's own business.

If the applicant has never borrowed from the bank, the lending officer will probably want to visit personally his place of business before making a credit decision. The importance of a visit to the borrower's plant should be emphasized.

In some banks, the credit department not only submits facts to the lending officer, but also its recommendations with reference to the extension of credit.

After the case has been analyzed by the credit department and referred back to the lending officer, if the amount involved exceeds his lending authority, or if he is at all doubtful about the proper decision, he should seek the group judgment of the officers' loan committee, or the directors' loan committee. Committee decisions should be encouraged on all doubtful cases since group judgment is usually superior to one man's decision.

If the maximum benefits of group judgment are to be obtained, the frank expression of dissenting opinions should be encouraged; otherwise the juniors are apt merely to adopt the opinions expressed by the senior members and the benefits of different opinions and group judgment will be lost to a large extent. It is not to be expected that committees will unanimously agree on all decisions and, where the committee is divided in its opinion, the decision of a majority should prevail.

The principal drawback to group judgment in loan decisions is the factor of delay. Borrowers usually want a prompt decision and after the required facts are made available, a prompt decision is expected and should be rendered. Nothing is more irritating to a borrower than to have his loan application delayed for several days while the lending officer is trying to get a decision from a loan committee. Borrowers have been known to withdraw very desirable loan applications because they became disgusted with waiting for a committee to act.

An officers' loan committee fulfills a useful function in many medium sized banks, since such a committee can hold frequent meetings and advise lending officers on doubtful cases. Many banks have daily meetings of the officers' loan committee. At such meetings, pending loan applications are reviewed, credit information exchanged, the preceding day's loans are announced, delinquent loans are discussed and assigned for follow-ups, and the next day's maturities are also discussed. There is a distinct need for such a committee in addition to the function of the directors' loan committee. Such a daily meeting offers many advantages.

Although promptness on loan decisions is something that all banks should strive for, it is foolhardy to attempt decisions until adequate information is available and has been considered by the appropriate persons. On new lines of credits and large loans, the borrower must be made to understand in the beginning that proper consideration of the loan will necessarily require time and that a decision cannot be expected immediately.

Once a decision is reached with reference to a loan, the decision must be loyally supported by the lending officer handling the loan even though he might personally have had a different opinion. It is a sign of poor organization when a lending officer tells a customer, "I strongly recommended your loan, but the committee declined it". The decision of the committee becomes the decision of the bank, and it is downright disloyalty to the institution for an officer to indicate to the customer that he disagrees with the committee's decision.

When it is necessary to decline a loan application, the officer or committee should have definite reasons and usually those reasons can be candidly expressed. It may require real salesmanship to convince a loan applicant that the bank was justified in declining the loan, but it is always worth the effort to attempt to justify the bank's position.

It is desirable to have all loans classified as to type at the time they are made, in order that statistical control can be maintained as to the volume of the various kinds of loans. Each loan should also be identified as to the approving officer so that loans may be grouped or totaled for report purposes according to the respective lending officers.

The Federal Reserve Board periodically calls for reports as to the volume of loans in various classifications, and it is a convenience to have controls which will readily permit this information to be prepared without having to make a special breakdown for this purpose.

Through proper accounting controls, it is possible to prepare reports showing exactly what types of loans are being made, which officers are making them, and which types of loans are producing the greatest earnings and the highest ratio of losses. It should be possible to give each lending officer each month a report showing his volume of loans in each classification, the average interest being earned on such loans, a statement of his delinquent loans, and a statement of chargeoffs or losses, if any. Through a study of such reports, the management can obtain a clear picture of just what is happening within the loan and discount department.

Within the framework of monetary management in bank operations, it is possible to find many expedient and valuable applications of loan classification.

During recent years, there has been a constantly increasing number of loan reports required by bank supervisory authorities. Unless the bank has a routine method of classifying these loans, the processing of the required data is laborious, expensive, and time-consuming, and upon completion the reports will possibly be inaccurate and unreliable. In addition to the reports required by supervisory authorities, routine reports on the status of bank loans are most desirable within the framework of the bank operations. These reports are simplified and expedited by good classification.

A good, sound classification system provides accurate and thorough knowledge of the loan portfolio. This information, in turn, enables the bank management to establish sound loan policies, based on this thorough knowledge of the portfolio.

Loan classification permits the segregation of the types of loans in the portfolio which in turn focuses the spotlight on loan concentrations. These concentrations can then be meticulously reviewed in order to prevent unnecessary exposure of the loss.

During recent years, it has become increasingly difficult for bank management to plan secondary reserves and the investment program, due to fluctuating deposits and an unprecedented demand for loans. Loan classification, when combined with historical experience, enables the management to project the possible loan demand volume over a six-month period. This projection, when combined with an analysis of the future deposit trends, should provide sound planning which will avoid forced liquidation of investments. With this data, the fiscal planners are enabled to translate the loan volume into future interest income, which also facilitates budgetary planning.

Many auxiliary aids also result from good classification systems. Through the use of this method, it is possible to establish the volume of paper eligible for rediscount with the Federal Reserve banks. The status of loan categories, such as real estate and construction loans can be checked against level limitations and departmental work loads can be determined.

Increasing the volume of sound loans in a commercial bank is a process that can best be done by indirect methods rather than direct. Loans cannot be sold by usual sales methods nor by high pressure tactics, but must be developed through orderly processes.

Neither a relaxation of lending standards nor an affirmative decision on all doubtful credit cases is the right approach toward a program for an increased amount of good loans. A satisfactory volume of loans is apt to be the natural by-product flowing from good organization, sound policies, thorough procedures, and competent personnel rather than aggressive solicitation or lax credit standards.

The first step toward obtaining more loans is for the bank to determine definitely just what specifications it will require on its loans. Unless the management, the lending officers and, to some extent, the customers have a clear understanding of the bank's loan policies, many desirable loans will never be consummated because of a lack of understanding by one or more of the parties. Once the bank's loan objectives are clearly established, it should be easier for all concerned to strive to achieve the goal.

After loan policies have been determined, the next requirement is competent personnel. This includes lending officers, credit investigators, analysts, and experienced supervisory personnel, working through committees or a senior officer. A well-informed and widely experienced lending staff can safely extend credit in more cases than the same number of loan officers of limited experience and ability. An alert, aggressive credit department can produce more information upon which lending officers can confidently rely in making loan decisions. Experienced supervisory personnel can frequently make suggestions which will enable a doubtful loan plan to be revised in a manner that will result in a sound credit.

Ignorance breeds suspicion. When lending officers are poorly informed, their credit decisions are more apt to be negative than in cases where a situation is fully understood. Therefore, before attempting to develop the maximum possibilities in loans and to adopt advisedly any policy other than so-called "riskless lending," a bank should be reasonably sure that it has a competent lending staff and credit organization.

Efficient loan and credit procedures permit prompt decisions, while loose organization and inefficient procedures are productive of delays which are apt to discourage borrowers and drive them elsewhere.

Modern banking has developed many devices in connection with its lending activities. Not all banks in the medium sized class have fully informed themselves or properly equipped the bank to take advantage of these various "tools of credit."

Even after a good lending and credit organization is established with clearly understood loan policies and smooth, efficient procedures, loans may not materialize in the volume desired, and a bank may have to go further in its loan efforts.

After the step of perfecting the lending organization internally has been satisfactorily accomplished, the next move is to tell the public about it. Do not brag about how good your bank is or how anxious you are to make loans, but tell the customer what you can do for *him*. Educate the public with reference to your loan policies in terms of what you have to offer. The average person is poorly informed as to what a bank will do and what it will not do in the matter of loans. The more widely the public is informed as to what a bank has to offer in the matter of credit, the more the public can be expected to use those facilities.

However effective advertising may be, it can go just so far and no farther. Even though a bank is efficiently organized in its lending activities and promulgates a satisfactory advertising program for loans, there is still much that can be done to develop additional loans.

It is the rule rather than the exception today in medium sized banks that the lending officers devote some portion of their time to calling upon the bank's customers. In many banks, each lending officer is expected to give a half day each week to such calls.

The value of those calls is undisputed. In the first place, the customer is invariably pleased and sometimes flattered that a bank officer voluntarily pays a visit and expresses appreciation for the business the bank has received. The bank officer, in return, can gain much valuable information about the customer and his business methods that he could never gain in any other manner.

Any well-rounded program for the development of loans should include a systematic plan for the lending officers to call upon the bank's larger customers and potential borrowers.

CHAPTER VIII

Installment Loans

PRIOR TO THE 1940's, commercial banks had not generally made monthly installment payment loans except in the real estate mortgage field, and monthly amortized mortgages were not common in commercial banks prior to 1934. Unsecured personal loans payable in monthly installments and monthly payment loans secured by automobiles did not gain widespread acceptance by commercial banks until after World War II. Since that time commercial banks have aggressively entered the installment loan field and it now appears that it is a well established and an important function of banking.

As in many other departments of banking, there is a complete lack of uniformity in terminology. For instance, such loans in commercial banks, are handled in departments variously designated, as: Installment Loan Department, Personal Loan Department, Consumer Credit Department, Time Payment Plan, Monthly Payment Department, and other similar names.

Generally speaking, this type of lending falls into two broad classes; direct lending where the bank deals with the borrower personally, and the wholesale function such as the purchase of dealer paper and notes and contracts from dealers and rediscounting for finance companies.

It should be recognized that while the fundamental principles of commercial bank lending and installment lending may be similar, there are differences which should be realized and understood. Balance sheets, profit and loss statements, and ratios have but little, if any significance in personal installment lending. The fundamental principles of installment lending are character, and ability of the borrower to repay. Installment lending men must be good judges of character and have a sort of "sixth sense" for misrepresentation. Above all, they must be interested in people and skilled in human relations.

Installment lending involves calculated risks and a conservative banker who tries to restrict such transactions to risk-proof loans will probably not be a success in this field of lending. Many commercial banks, in a desire to obtain lending men with the right philosophy of lending for personal installment loans, have employed men with previous lending experience with the "major finance companies" such as General Motors Acceptance Corporation and Universal Credit Corporation.

It is believed that experience with a finance company or in retail credit is a better background for the Installment Loan Department than commercial banking loans. Many installment loan men also feel that young men under 40 are better installment loan interviewers than older men. This is based on the theory that older men are more apt to be awe-inspiring, and harder to confide in than younger men. This is a cliche that is difficult of proof, but it seems reasonable.

One bank that has been very successful in training installment loan interviewers, carefully selects promising young men for this position and begins their training by assigning delinquent installment accounts to them for collection under the supervision of an experienced collection man. The collection of delinquent accounts is an effective way to observe and learn the pitfalls and mistakes of installment lending. The second phase of training might well be interviewing personal loan applicants, referring all except the obviously good secured loans to a senior for a decision.

Bank officers and directors responsible for policies of the Personal Loan Department (or whatever name the department handling installment loans to individuals is called), must recognize that in the very nature of such business there will be some losses. The higher rates of interest charged on such loans should compensate for such losses, as well as the relatively high accounting costs. So long as such losses are in reasonable proportion to the volume they should be accepted philosophically as inevitable. Some banks regard 1/2 of 1% of loans consummated as a reasonable loss ratio, while other banks expect a higher loss ratio in this division of lending.

One prominent installment lending man has stated that he can turn the losses in his department off and on like a faucet, by tightening or relaxing the lending policy. By shutting off losses altogether, it will necessarily restrict the volume and lower profits. Relaxing standards increases volume, but also increases losses. A middle-of-the-road course, or happy medium which recognizes that loans will not be limited to air-tight, riskless cases, but will include prudent risks which will probably result in some losses, will produce greater net profits than the super-conservative policy which seeks to avoid all losses.

Installment loan departments should systematically set aside a certain portion of gross income collected, say from five to ten per cent of gross income, as a reserve for losses. The fact that such a reserve exists makes it easier to maintain a liberal charge off policy and takes some of the sting out of loan mistakes which are certain to occur.

There are conflicting policies and theories with respect to charging off doubtful and slow personal loans. Conservative banking and accounting suggests charging off a loan as soon as it is as much as 60 days delinquent. The conflicting theory is that a charged off loan is not followed for collection as diligently as a loan on the current ledger.

A reasonable compromise between these two theories is to place the responsibility for pursuing collection of a loan for the first 60 days of delinquency on the lending man who originated the loan. At the end of 60 days, unless immediate collection seems assured, the loan should be charged off for accounting purposes, but placed in the hands of a collection specialist who will diligently pursue collection until he has been relieved of that duty by responsible authority. After the delinquent loan has been turned over to the collection specialist, all contacts with the borrower should be handled by him to avoid misunderstandings and confusion.

In any bank with a sizable volume of personal installment loans, the services of a full time outside field man for the vigorous pursuit of delinquent payments is regarded as a necessity.

In discussing record systems of personal installment loan departments, it is to be assumed that in all cases both the originating, collecting, and accounting in connection with such loans, is handled in a separate department rather than being handled in the regular Loan and Discount Department of a commercial bank.

There are many valid arguments for operating the Personal Installment Loan Department as a more or less autonomous group. In the first place, the philosophy of

96

such lending varies from ordinary commercial banking so that it prudently requires lending men with a somewhat different outlook from the typical commercial banker.

Secondly, the nature of the business and the probable large number of loan applicants usually makes it desirable to have separate physical quarters from the other loan departments of the bank. Such departments have often found it expedient to adopt different banking hours from the commercial loan department, and this also makes separate quarters desirable.

It is desirable to have the loan cages and accounting records of installment loans adjacent to the lending interviewers and this also points to the desirability of separate accounting facilities.

The accounting records and procedures in installment lending are customarily somewhat different from conventional commercial bank lending records. There are numerous good systems and accounting machines which are well adapted to such installment loans. Some of these systems are splendid for a small department with perhaps from three to five thousand accounts, but are impractical and inadequate for a ten to fifteen thousand account department. In designing or adopting an accounting system for an installment loan department, it is important to bear in mind that the volume may expand rapidly and the system, the machines and procedures should be such as to be adaptable to rapid expansion. Another principle to bear in mind is that it is a volume business which requires speed in handling individual items, and each clerk or teller must handle a heavy volume in more or less routine fashion.

In addition to the usual accounting controls for the purposes of accuracy and balancing, it is important that an adequate system of classification of loans by type and maturity is possible. Such statistical control permits management to be constantly aware of the volume of each classification of loan, the allocation of the loans to the various lending men, the types of loans that prove troublesome and result in losses, and an overall statistical picture of the department. Such statistical reports are very important to top management in evaluating the operations of the installment loan department and in the determination of its policies.

It is difficult to establish hard and fast rules to be rigidly observed in making personal loans to be repaid out of income, but there are many "rules of thumb" which men experienced in this field of lending believe are generally true and should be borne in mind even though such rules may sometimes be prudently waived.

Some of these so-called "rules of thumb," or recommended policies and procedures, are as follows:

1. Personal loan applications should be a simplified form more in the nature of a questionnaire rather than the balance sheet statement form for individuals used by Federal Reserve member banks. It is a good policy to have the borrower make the representations upon which the loan is based in an application in his own handwriting, and signed by him.

This procedure is desirable for several reasons:

a. The borrower will not be as glib in his written statements as he might be orally and he will probably hesitate to obtain a loan based upon a written misrepresentation.

b. If the loan application is in the borrower's own handwriting, it prevents the lending interviewer from "polishing it up" to justify his affirmative credit decision.

98

c. Such a record is valuable in appraising the quality of loans, and in the event of default, to attempt to determine if the cause of the delinquency could have been foreseen.

2. Although prompt decisions are desirable on personal loans, such decision on new and unknown borrowers should be delayed until the facts stated in the borrower's application have been verified. The greater the haste of the borrower, the more cautious the lender should be. Beware of the borrower who won't give the bank time to investigate and verify.

3. Beware of the borrower who wishes to conceal the fact of the loan from his wife. Domestic discord is one of the recognized hazards of personal lending, and it is a danger sign.

4. Don't make loans to alcoholics or persons known to be intemperate drinkers. Such situations often lead to other difficulties and collection troubles.

5. The fact that the applicant has been a long time with the same employer is a good credit sign. Be careful of the loan applicant who is in a new job, or has a record of changing jobs often.

6. Certain occupations seem to be better credit risks than others. These occupations probably differ in various sections of the country, but a shrewd analyst of personal credits can often detect an occupational pattern. Beware of the applicants in your community who, as occupational groups, seem to be sub-standard in meeting their financial obligations.

7. The purpose of the loan is perhaps more important in personal loans than in commercial lending. If the purpose seems extravagant in proportion to the borrower's income, it is a danger sign. Loans for the consolidation of existing debts often indicate extravagance and poor fi-

nancial management in the past. A loan for such purposes should be very cautiously examined.

8. Direct personal loans to purchasers of new automobiles are perhaps the most attractive and profitable types of personal installment loans. The fundamental principles to bear in mind on such loans are:

a. The assured income of the borrower must be apparently sufficient that he can meet the payments without too much difficulty.

b. The amount of the loan must be in proper proportion to the dealers cost and the amortization schedule should be such that the borrower will have a substantial equity in the car.

c. Adequate insurance coverage in favor of the lender.

d. The borrower must not only have an adequate income but a good past record for paying his obligations promptly.

9. Loans on used cars can also be made successfully if the above principles of lending on new cars are observed and the lender does not make the mistake of lending "too much and for too long."

The wholesale division of installment lending (sometimes called "dealer installment loans") is concerned with the purchase or rediscount of paper originated by other lenders.

Since under normal circumstances all of the underlying credits or collateral in such a department originate with others outside the bank's own organization, the most important function is the selection and policing of the dealers or others to whom credit is extended by this department.

In approving the dealers whose paper will be accepted, the fundamental principles of credit, including the three "C's" of Character, Capital, and Capacity, must be observed. Although character is of paramount importance in any loan, it is doubly significant in dealer paper, since in indirect lending there are so many possibilities involving fraud and misrepresentation.

Adequate capital to handle the volume of business undertaken and earning capacity sufficient to discharge liabilities that may be incurred, are likewise important in approving dealers.

Dealer paper is usually purchased with full recourse on the dealer and with the understanding that the debtor on the underlying paper will be notified. Such notification should be given by the purchasing bank, and promptly. Thereafter, all payments should be made to the bank. Although it is desirable to have the dealer interested and co-operative, he should not be allowed to receive collections on such paper nor make payments in the name of the debtor.

The outstandings of each dealer should be segregated so that the contingent liability is known and controlled at all times.

While it is usually impracticable for the bank to attempt to make a credit examination on each item of paper purchased from a dealer, it is prudent and advisable to "sample test" a representative portion of such paper at intervals to appraise the quality. One method of sampling sometimes employed for this purpose is to obtain a credit report on every tenth case.

Since the quality of each individual case cannot be examined, the bank, to a considerable degree, will have to rely upon the delinquency record and the over-all results to judge the quality of the dealer's paper.

Unless the dealer has established financial responsibility to the extent that he is entitled to the full line of credit on an unsecured basis (and such cases are rare), it is prudent to require a substantial dealers reserve to indemnify his potential liability. Such reserves should be based on a percentage of the outstandings and may be adjusted upward or downward from time to time as the experience with the dealer seems to indicate.

One of the difficult phases of dealer paper lending is that it often involves and requires "floor planning". Floor planning, of course, is the use of chattels such as automobiles, appliances, road or farm machinery, or other such items as collateral with the pledged collateral remaining in the possession of the dealer. The laws of the various states differ as to the status of the legal title to such pledged personal property, but even though the equities as between the dealer and the bank are well established in law, if the pledged property gets into the possession of an innocent purchaser for value, the bank usually loses its lien and right to possession.

Floor planning, therefore, in its very nature requires careful supervision and policing to make certain that the specific pledged property remains in the possession of the dealer and that it is properly marked or identified to denote the bank's lien or title. Some types of property, such as automobiles which have clearly established serial numbers, and can easily be identified and verified, are much better adapted to floor planning than other items which may not have serial numbers, and are difficult to count and identify.

Some bankers regard floor planning as a necessary nuisance which must be accepted in order to get dealer paper.

If a bank decides to engage in floor planning, it should do so with the full realization that to be properly administered and policed, it will require constant and frequent checks of the pledged property by the bank's own representatives. Such inspections are, of course, expensive from the bank's viewpoint and necessitate interest charges and service fees commensurate with the administrative expense.

The rediscounting of notes for finance companies is a somewhat different procedure from the purchase of dealer paper, but many of the principles involved are similar, as in the case of dealers the integrity and efficiency of the finance company must be carefully examined and appraised. Managerial ability and the quality of the paper offered is tremendously important. Complete records as to the current status of each obligation pledged must be maintained by the bank, and frequent reconciliation must be made between the bank's records and the borrower's books. It is obvious that the volume of records and the necessity of reconciliations will occasion considerable administrative expense which must be taken into consideration in determining the basis on which finance company paper can be profitably rediscounted.

Good statistical control and constant scrutiny are required by banks in supervising indirect installment lending. Such lines of credit which have been satisfactory for a long time may change quickly, and the bank must be prompt to detect unfavorable changes and close out the account if necessary. The supervision of this type of lending is a position requiring experience in this particular field of lending, good sound judgment, and the courage to act quickly and firmly when the situation demands it.

Installment lending by banks in both direct loans and in taking paper originated by others can be a sound, profitable business, but it is full of pitfalls and requires a specialist well trained in this field.

NEW TYPES OF INSTALLMENT CREDIT

The notable success of bank consumer credit financing has influenced many banks to go a step further. Thus, there has emerged the newest type of consumer financing: Charge account plan and revolving personal loans, sometimes known as the Check-credit plan.

Although there is a basic similarity in the operation of both type plans, each is designed for a specific purpose and is discussed separately. Both plans provide the customer with a "line of credit" to be used at his discretion and to be repaid in a flexible manner.

CHARGE ACCOUNT PLAN

The charge account plan operates primarily through merchants, and is designed to provide a service for the merchant as well as the customer. Basically, this plan provides a means by which the customers previously approved by the bank, make charge purchases from a member merchant who, in turn, sells these charge accounts to the bank for immediate cash. There are several variations of the plan. One widely used, accomplishes these purchases by use of a distinctive credit card issued the customer by the bank and honored by participating merchants.

The term "merchant" as used in connection with charge account plans should be interpreted broadly and should include proprietors of business firms, service companies, or even professional men, who are not merchants in the usual sense of the word. Many service organizations such as shoe repair shops, automobile repair shops, and other such businesses are frequently "member merchants" in charge account plans.

The customer makes written application for a credit card. The application form, which is signed by the customer, contains not only pertinent credit information, but also indicates the customer's agreement to the terms of the charge account plan. After satisfactory credit investigation, the bank issues the credit card, usually a plastic card imprinted with the customer's name, address, and a card number. The customer is assigned a credit limit, or "line of credit." He is then free to make charge purchases from participating merchants up to his line of credit. All charge purchases made by use of the card are sold to the bank by the member merchant, and once each month the customer receives a statement from the bank covering all such purchases. The customer then has the option of paying all such charges within 30 days from his billing date without charge—or he may elect to pay only a specified minimum portion of these purchases and carry the remainder to the next month. He pays a service charge, usually 1%, per month, on the balance of his account carried forward.

The merchant who wishes to become a participant or "member merchant" under the charge account plan also makes application to the bank. An investigation of the merchant is made and if acceptable, the bank enters into a written agreement with the merchant, setting forth the terms and conditions under which it will purchase charge sales made by cardholders. The merchant is charged a discount or "service charge" on each charge ticket purchased. This discount is normally 5% to 6%. The merchant receives immediate credit in his checking account for charge sales so purchased. All such purchases are on a non-recourse basis, except where disputed accounts are involved.

This plan offers the customer several advantages: first, convenience. All purchases from several stores appear on one bill. Only one payment is necessary. Second, the plan affords the customer a great flexibility in manner of repayment. Third, the customer is relieved of the necessity of carrying cash. The one credit card is honored at many stores of varied types.

The plan benefits the member merchant in a number of ways. First, he receives immediate cash for his credit sales. Second, he is relieved of all credit and collection problems. Third, he, as a member of the plan, has a large potential of good customers. All cardholders are his good potential customers.

Many charge account plans provide an additional "instant cash" feature. This feature permits a cardholder to present his charge card to a bank teller, sign a simple note form, and obtain cash up to the amount of his credit limit.

There are several advantages to the bank in this plan. It attracts new customers for the bank and new deposits. It provides a new and useful service to the business community and increases good will. Once established, it is profitable on a volume basis.

Disadvantages of the charge account plan are:

It requires a rather large initial investment in promotional expense, equipment and personnel. The plan normally is not profitable for the first two to three years.

Operation of such a plan is a departure from conventional banking credit standards and philosophy. Loss percentages usually run higher than bank installment loans. Past due ratios are also higher.

There is a sizable volume of items to be handled in the plan. Monthly statements showing detailed charges must be billed and mailed to many accounts.

For banks considering starting such a plan, there are several do's and don'ts offered for guidance.

Do be certain of the wholehearted and enthusiastic cooperation of your Board of Directors and bank staff before embarking.

Do be prepared to allow an ample budget for promotional expense. This is one of the larger costs of starting the plan. You must sell the public something new and unknown.

Do get a person to supervise the operation who is familiar with retail credits. A credit manager of a large department store often makes an excellent manager.

Do seek the cooperation and acceptance of the plan by the merchants. They can make or break the plan.

Do plan on losses.

Don'ts of the plan are as follows:

Don't plan on the operation's making a substantial profit in less than three years.

Don't set credit standards for cardholders too high. Remember you must use retail merchant credit standards—not bank standards.

Don't pursue exacting and drastic collection methods. The customer who pays his department store account slowly, but regularly is regarded as a good customer.

Don't worry about losses running high the first year of operation. It takes this long for the shakedown cruise. Initially, you may knowingly approve some sub-marginal credit risks in order to sell the merchants on the plan.

CHECK-CREDIT PLAN

The check-credit plan enables a customer to write checks up to an agreed credit limit. These checks, although distinctive to the bank for internal operational purposes, can be used in exactly the same manner as personal checks. Instead of being charged against a regular checking account, they are posted to the customer's check-credit account. The customer has an option of repayment plans, and each payment to his account restores that amount of credit. A monthly service charge, usually 1%, is made on the amount of credit used each month. There is also a small charge for each check written, usually 25c.

In most banks operating the check credit plan, customers desiring such credit make a written application for a definite amount of credit, and after due investigation, the customer who is accepted signs a contract with the bank in which he agrees to the terms and conditions of the plan. These terms include the amount of service charge and usually provide for payments of either 1/20th of the total of his line of credit or 1/10th the amount actually owing, whichever is lesser. Normally, a minimum payment of $10.00 is required. Once this contract is signed, no other instrument or evidence of indebtedness is necessary. The loan simply continues to revolve. Checks drawn by the customer and monthly service charges are entered as charges; all payments are credits.

This plan is advantageous to the customer for several reasons. First, he has a line of credit available to use as he desires. Second, the plan is convenient. Once set up, there is no need for the customer to come in to the bank again. The contract does not need renewing. Third, the customer has a choice of payments; and fourth, he only pays a service charge on amounts he actually uses.

One word of caution to banks entering this type credit. Greater selectivity and closer credit screening is necessary in this plan than the charge account plan. Lines of credit are usually larger and it is completely unsecured. It is necessary that some type review system be adopted, since there is no maturity. However, the bank's internal operation of this plan is much simpler than that of the charge account plan.

CHAPTER IX

Real Estate Mortgage Loans

．

IN DISCUSSING REAL ESTATE LENDING it might be well to consider the basic concepts of a mortgage loan. Of course, a real estate mortgage loan is obviously a secured loan. We sometimes speak of the real estate securing the loan, but it is to be observed that the security is an interest in real estate, and not the real estate itself, since the lender has only a latent, or passive interest in the real estate prior to a default in the mortgage. In a typical collateral loan secured by a pledge of personal property, there is usually a provision that additional security will be furnished the lender upon demand if the value of the security originally pledged declines. This is not usually true in real estate lending, and once real estate security is accepted, if the value declines, the lender has no rights to demand additional security.

Of course, in lending money secured by real estate, the market value of the real estate at the time of the loan is expected to provide a margin over and above the amount of the loan that will protect the loan during its term against all contingencies. The extent of this margin of safety is discussed later in this chapter.

In making mortgage loans, the lender should have a full understanding that land is owned subject to the following rights of the government:

1. The right of eminent domain, or seizure by governmental bodies for public use.
2. The police power of the state and municipality, that is, the right of the governmental authorities to control the use of the land.
3. The right of the state to levy *ad valorem* and improvement taxes on the property.

These inherent rights of the government frequently affect the value of property and can adversely affect a mortgagee's interest.

The adequacy and marketability of the property pledged as security are of primary importance in a mortgage loan and the probability (or perhaps lack of probability) of default is likewise an important factor. Even though the security is adequate, if the ability of the borrower to meet the required payments appears doubtful, or if the borrower's record for taking care of his financial obligations is unfavorable, banks do not normally approve such loans since foreclosure is an undesirable method of liquidating a loan.

There have been a number of systems established for rating the quality of mortgage loans. These plans usually involve the rating of the borrower, the rating of the property, and the rating of the neighbourhood surrounding the mortgaged property. Some of these rating plans are complex and involve quite a number of estimates. The summary of such ratings is frequently referred to as the "mortgage pattern."

110

In making a decision on a mortgage loan application, there are two distinct fields of inquiry. First, the borrower must be appraised and, second, the property offered as security must be appraised. Everyone connected with credits and lending in a bank is familiar with the "Three C's" of credit—Character, Capacity, and Capital, and in mortgage lending, as in all other types of loans, the character of the borrower is of paramount importance. Unless the borrower has the willingness and desire to meet his just obligations as they mature and his past conduct reflects a satisfactory record in this respect, then the decision should be negative, and the investigation need go no further. There is a tendency by some to rely too much upon appraised values, and not enough on pertinent facts regarding the borrower's ability to pay.

Since most mortgage loans under present day conditions are for an extended term, and loans of ten, fifteen, and even twenty-five years are not unusual, it is pertinent to look at the borrower's age in such long term loan applications and consider whether he is likely to have the sustained earning power or income during the proposed term of the mortgage to take care of the scheduled payments.

Another factor to be considered is whether or not the proposed loan is in the borrower's best interest, irrespective of whether he has the ability to pay. Some instances of this sort have been encountered in G.I. applications for homes where unreasonably high selling prices have been quoted, and a bank could not, in good faith, be a party to a transaction where obviously the borrower and purchaser were being victimized.

Once the bank has satisfied itself as to the borrower, the property offered as security to the mortgage loan should be carefully appraised. Numerous textbooks have been written on real estate appraisals. It is not an exact science and a real estate appraisal is nothing more than an opinion of value at the time it is made. The worth of such an opinion, to some extent, depends upon the appraiser's knowledge of the principles of appraising, his familiarity with current values and prices, and his knowledge of the history of real estate in the particular vicinity. Any appraiser who has not experienced a severe real estate depression can hardly realize the extent to which prices may be depressed.

"Market value" is defined by the American Institute of Real Estate Appraisers as being that amount of money a property will yield at a·sale if exposed to the market for a reasonable period of time with both the buyer and the seller being fully informed as to all of the uses of the property and with neither buyer nor seller being under any compulsion to buy or sell.

There is no such thing as "normal value" as to real estate since real estate values may fluctuate as widely as commodities and securities and no one can accurately forecast the extent of future value trends. The value of buildings may be established with greater certainty than the value of land, for the reason that, although no particular spot of land may be exactly reproduced, the reproduction cost of any building may be mathematically computed. Experienced appraisers attempt to keep well informed on current building costs, and can estimate the cost of any building on a square foot basis, or a cubic foot basis. This method may be reasonably accurate for new buildings, but in older buildings the depreciation and obsolescence factors must be reckoned with, and this involves a second estimate.

There are three recognized methods of estimating real estate market values and each method can be used and be combined with the others to effectively determine the present market value of a specific parcel of real estate. Perhaps the most common and widely used method is the cost approach which consists of estimating the cost to duplicate the subject property by acquiring a comparable plot of land and erecting duplicate improvements. This becomes more difficult in older buildings as the improvements must be depreciated due to physical deterioration, functional obsolescence, and economic obsolescence, but these items can be effectively measured by well qualified appraisers.

A second approach to value is obtained by estimating the income the property is capable of producing and by capitalizing the net income into value.

A third method is the comparison of actual sales prices of similar properties and adjusting these sales prices to the property in question.

An appraiser should use all of these approaches in forming an opinion of value and then choose the measure of value which he believes is most accurate in the particular case under consideration. If the three methods are perfectly applied, then the figures obtained should be exactly the same; however, this rarely happens, as there are a number of different estimates included in each method. If there is a difference of more than 15% in any of the three calculations, then it is likely that at least one approach has been misapplied, and the data should be carefully examined again.

Sometimes real estate is offered as security for mortgage loans and the buildings on the land are suitable only for a "special purpose" or for very limited purposes. In such cases the reconstruction cost, or cost less depreciation method cannot be used as a measure of value unless due allowance is made for the estimated cost of converting the buildings to a more general purpose which will make the property readily salable. In the case of a building erected for special purposes, and which can be used for only certain limited purposes, full value cannot be prudently allowed. It is likewise true that if a building, particularly a dwelling, is not suitable to its location, the reproduction cost must be discounted. We sometimes speak of property being "overbuilt"—that is to say, the building is too fine for the neighbourhood, meaning that an average purchaser would not be willing to pay full cost value at that location.

In most banks, one or more of the officers are usually real estate appraisers. If a bank does not have this type of experience within its own staff, then it is only prudent to employ a competent, disinterested appraiser to make appraisals for real estate lending. Especially on larger loans it is desirable to have the opinion of a disinterested, outside party, even though the bank may have experienced appraisers within the bank.

In selecting an outside appraiser, it is important to judge his qualifications, training, experience, clientele, and professional designations. Banks sometimes engage several appraisers to appraise properties that are to be offered for sale and then note the actual sales price obtained as compared with the appraised values to see how accurately the appraisers have estimated the market value. It is not uncommon for any appraiser to miss a sales price by from 5% to 10%, but an appraiser who cannot usually estimate market values within this range is of little use to a lending institution. Some institutions will accept only members of The American Institute of Real Estate Appraisers as evaluators. This organization has extremely high standards of training and experience and does not accept individuals who have not proven their ability as appraisers. The Institute has a very rigid code of ethics which members must follow. There are of course many well qualified appraisers who do not belong to The American Institute of Appraisers, but the members of that group are certain to be experienced and well trained.

A word of caution might be appropriate with reference to mortgage loans to institutions such as churches, hospitals, schools, etc. Churches are frequently seekers of mortgage credit, and such mortgage applications must be carefully scrutinized. As a matter of public relations, a bank may offend many of its good customers by declining a church loan, and yet many proposed church loans are essentially unsound. A church building is usually a "special purpose" building of the highest degree. There is every reason why a bank would shrink from foreclosing on a church building, and if foreclosure is completed, the foreclosed property is more than apt to have an extremely limited market, regardless of its original cost. The income of a church is known to fluctuate widely according to business and economic conditions, and churches which engage in extensive building projects at times when their members are prosperous, are frequently unable to keep up their obligations in times of depression. The membership of churches is not static, but constantly changing, and the character of the management is therefore not stable from year to year. In times of depression, when church income is low, it is sometimes hard for a lender who holds a mortgage on the church to get the church members to consider seriously the church's debt when the members are having financial troubles of their own. What is everybody's business is frequently nobody's business. It is not uncommon for churches to offer to have several of the prominent and well-to-do members endorse the church's obligation. While endorsements of this character do strengthen the lender's possibilities of recovery, it must be recognized that accommodation endorsers usually avoid the payment of the debts of others insofar as it is possible, and recovery under such circumstances is usually distasteful, as well as difficult.

What has been said with reference to churches is usually true to some extent with reference to hospitals, clubs, schools, and other such institutions. While it cannot be said that institutional mortgage loans are never desirable, nevertheless, as a class they frequently prove troublesome, and such loan applications should be handled with the greatest caution.

Although the fundamental principles of mortgage lending may not have changed appreciably throughout the years, nevertheless customs and practices with reference to mortgage lending have undergone a wide change since 1930. Prior to the depression in the early thirties, relatively short-term loans—that is, 3 to 5 years—were the most popular type, and amortized loans were the exception rather than the rule. Under the old plan, a loan was made for a three or five year period, and neither the lender nor the borrower had the slightest expectation that the loan would be paid in full when due. Both fully expected that when the loan matured, it would probably be reduced if convenient to the borrower, and the principal balance extended or, if the lender needed his money at maturity, then the borrower would be expected to refinance the loan somewhere else. With the birth of the HOLC and the FHA, a new pattern of mortgage lending, particularly with reference to home loans began to appear. The loans were for a longer term with monthly amortization payments. This served to increase the length of the loan, but is more realistic since the borrower is expected to make the monthly payments out of income, and the plan does not provide for a lump sum principal payment which the borrower has no apparent means of paying. Monthly amortized loans have also inaugurated a higher percentage of loan values than formerly prevailed.

Prior to 1930, 50% of the current value was considered by many banks to be a maximum loan on residential property, although banking regulations permitted loans up to 60%. With the inauguration of FHA Title II loans, loans of 80% of the market value of the security were offered for the first time, and under certain types of loans on new construction 90% could be obtained. In justification of these liberal loans, it was stated in the beginning that these loans were being made during the depression at unprecedented low levels, but as values have inflated, no apparent attempt has been made to hold down the ratio of loans to security. It is easy to see that a slight error in appraisal or judgment, or a moderate slump in values, is certain to bring trouble to loans where the margin of safety is so thin. It must also be borne in mind that taxes and improvement assessments come ahead of a mortgage lien. Also, that the expense of foreclosure must be added to the mortgage debt. Therefore, it is not surprising that the amount of the debt at foreclosure is frequently considerably higher than the original amount of the mortgage loan.

Regardless of what bankers may think of governmental, subsidized lending, bankers generally should recognize that the Federal Government has taught bankers a sound lesson in home lending through the channels of the Federal Hous-

117

ing Administration. Although in some instances the plan may have been abused, and appraisals and terms of loans may have been too liberal, nevertheless, the plan of measuring the borrower's income and capacity to pay, and devising a contract of monthly payments whereby the borrower can pay principal, interest, taxes, and hazard insurance in monthly instalments, is a sound plan, and much better in most cases than short-term loans, or medium-term loans with a "balloon note" at final maturity.

For some years prior to 1930, from 6% to 8% was the prevailing rate on residential mortgage loans, 6 1/2% being the prevailing rate about 1930. After the mortgage paralysis in early 1930, when mortgage lending was resumed, 5% became the prevailing rate, and this rate later was reduced to 4 1/2%, and then to 4%. At least these rates applied in the larger cities. Since then, the trend has been reversed, and 5% to 6% is again the prevailing rate.

Section 24 of the Federal Reserve Act provides that mortgage loans of national banks shall not exceed 50 per centum of the appraised value of the real estate offered as security and no such loan shall be made for a longer term than five years; except that (1) any such loan may be made in an amount not to exceed 66-2/3 per centum of the appraised value of the real estate offered as security and for a term not longer than ten years if the loan is secured by an amortized mortgage, deed or trust, or other such instrument under the terms of which the installment payments are sufficient to amortize 40 per centum or more of the principal of the loan within a period of not more than ten years, (2) any such loan may be made in an amount not to exceed 66-2/3 per centum of the appraised value of the real estate offered as security and for a term not longer than twenty years if the loan is secured by an amortized

118

mortgage, deed of trust, or other such instrument under the terms of which the installment payments are sufficient to amortize the entire principal of the loan within a period of not more than twenty years, and (3) any such loan may be made in an amount not to exceed 75 per centum of the appraised value of the real estate offered as security and for a term not longer than 20 years if the loan is secured by an amortized mortgage, deed of trust, or other such instrument under the terms of which the installment payments are sufficient to amortize the entire principal of the loan within the period ending on the date of its maturity, and (4) the foregoing limitations and restrictions shall not prevent the renewal or extension of loans heretofore made and shall not apply to real estate loans which are insured under the provisions of title II, title VI, title VIII, section 8 of title I, or title IX of the National Housing Act, or which are insured by the Secretary of Agriculture pursuant to title I of the Bankhead-Jones Farm Tenant Act, or the Act entitled "An Act to promote conservation in the arid and semiarid areas of the United States by aiding in the development of facilities for water storage and utilization, and for other purposes," approved August 28, 1937, as amended, and shall not apply to real estate loans which are fully guaranteed or insured by a State, or by a State authority for the payment of the obligations of which the faith and credit of the State is pledged, if under the terms of the guaranty or insurance agreement the association will be assured of repayment in accordance with the terms of the loan. No national banking association shall make such loans in an aggregate sum in excess of the amount of the capital stock of such association paid in and unimpaired plus the amount of its unimpaired surplus fund, or in excess of 60 per centum of the amount of its time and savings deposits, whichever is the greater.

The practice of many banks in making mortgage loans, has usually been to have a local practicing attorney examine an abstract of title to the property offered as security, and certify to the lender that the borrower has a good, merchantable title to the property, and that the proposed mortgage in favor of the lender will constitute a valid first lien. While most banks have found this practice reasonably satisfactory, it is to be noted that the value of such an opinion depends upon the professional ability of the attorney in question and, in the event the title later proves faulty, the financial responsibility of the certifying attorney may determine whether or not the bank will suffer a loss through the failure of title. In recent years, the practice of obtaining title insurance from reputable title companies has gained wide favor. Title insurance is particularly important where there is a possibility that the lender may want to find a secondary market for the mortgage, and offer it for sale, or as security for a loan. In such a case, title insurance will make the mortgage more readily marketable than the opinion of a local attorney.

In addition to a certificate of title, it is prudent to obtain a surveyor's certificate that the improvements on the property are within the boundaries of the mortgaged property, and that there are no encroachments.

In summarizing the above principles, the following should be emphasized:

1. The general standing and the moral and financial responsibility of the borrower.
2. The apparent ability of the borrower to meet the payments when due.
3. The value of the property offered as security, bear-

ing in mind possible fluctuations in real estate values.

4. The desirability of steady amortization of the debt.
5. That the borrower has a good, merchantable title, and that the mortgage will constitute a valid first lien.

If these principles are adhered to, there are few investments that are as essentially sound as first mortgage real estate loans.

CHAPTER X

Investments

THERE IS PERHAPS MORE DIVERSITY in the size and form of the investment organization of a medium sized bank than in the other major departments. This diversity results in the widely different functions that may or may not be performed in connection with investments.

For instance, a bank that performs the function of a securities dealer and engages in underwriting and trading in government and municipal securities to the extent permitted by banking regulations obviously will require a more extensive investment organization than a bank that does not engage in such activities.

In the larger banks that have a sizable personal trust business the Trust Department usually has its own investment division which is frequently entirely separate from the bank's investment department, but in some medium sized banks with trust departments, the investment department also serves the trust department as well as servicing the bank's own investments and trading account.

Regardless of the departmental organization, it is a

primary requisite and fundamental principle that must always be observed that the bank must avoid any indirect as well as direct self-dealing insofar as trust funds are concerned.

There are valid arguments, both pro and con, for having the investment department in a medium sized bank supervise trust investments as well as the bank's own investments. This is a decision that will necessarily have to be decided in each individual bank in the light of the nature and volume of the investment matters it handles, and the experience and investment qualifications of the available personnel.

It is interesting to observe that one medium sized bank combined the functions of investment analysis and credit analysis in one department on the theory that the analysis of financial statements in connection with corporate securities, is closely analogous to the analysis of such statements for making loans to corporations. The practice of combining these functions in one department is not widespread, however, except in very small banks where the officers perform all functions and are not specialized.

In a medium sized bank that does not engage in investment underwriting or trading, and does not have a sizable personal trust department, primary responsibility for the investment function is usually vested in one of the senior officers who also has other responsibilities such as administrative duties and lending.

Other functions that are frequently performed by the investment department of a medium sized bank include investment advice and statistical service to customers, both individuals and small correspondent banks, buying and selling securities as agent for customers, and handling the sale and redemption of United States Savings Bonds.

It is obvious that any medium sized bank must necessarily depend upon outside sources for much of its investment information and advice rather than its own research facilities. There is available a wealth of investment information from the statistical services (such as Moody's, Standard-Poor, Fitch), as well as correspondent banks in the large financial centers. Investment dealers and brokers will supply banks with investment information and advice, but it is not prudent for a bank to permit a seller of securities to make investment decisions, or select securities for the bank. The bank officers must make independent decisions with respect to its investments, and it is a responsibility that cannot be delegated to outsiders, however expert they may be.

In the chapter on "Lending" the desirability of written loan policies was discussed and emphasized. Most of the same reasons that make written loan policies desirable are equally applicable to investment policies. The Board of Directors is responsible for the broad investment policies of a bank and the officers who actually carry out the investment policies should do so within the framework determined by the Board. The only way to make certain that the investment policies are understood by both the Board and the investment officers is to reduce such policies to writing. It should be the responsibility of the principal investment officer to review any such written statement of investment policies frequently, and call it to the Board's attention if any change of policy is desirable. The Board, of its own initiative, should also review the investment policies periodically.

Among the matters that might be covered in a bank's written statement of investment policy, are:

1. The goal of the investment program.

2. The size of the investment portfolio expressed in percentages as to U. S. Government bonds, the securities of states, cities, and other governmental units, etc.
3. The diversification of the portfolio as to non-governmental securities.
4. The diversification of the portfolio with respect to maturities.
5. The extent to which securities may be purchased for trading or resale.
6. The manner in which capital gains and losses resulting from investments shall be treated.
7. Specifying the person or persons who shall be authorized to purchase or sell securities for the bank's account.
8. Prescribing the procedures for the physical custody of bank-owned securities, including the pledging of securities where permitted or required by law.
9. Outlining a program of periodical review of the investment portfolio.

While investment policies will appropriately vary in different banks, there are some fundamental principles of bank investment policy that should be common to every bank:

a. The credit quality of the investments must be high.

b. All bank-owned securities must be readily marketable to insure liquidity.

c. Maturities should be prudently spaced with predominantly short maturities.

d. Diversification as to (1) geographical areas, (2) industries, (if corporate securities are included), and (3) maturities, should be followed to avoid undue concentration of risks.

e. Quality and maturity should never be ignored to obtain yield.

If a bank decides to have its investment policies reduced to writing, and approved by the board of directors, the following type of policy statement may be used:

Investment Policies

The following investment policies are established by The Blank National Bank for the guidance of all concerned.

The purpose of this statement of policies is to fix responsibilities for determining what portion of the bank's assets shall be invested in securities, the types of securities that shall be purchased, and the principles to be followed in buying and selling securities for the bank's investment account.

There shall be established a committee designated as the "Conversion Committee" which shall be composed of the bank's comptroller, the vice president in charge of the Investment department, and the senior lending officer. The Conversion Committee shall perform and be responsible for the functions and activities hereafter outlined.

It shall be the function and duty of the Conversion Committee to maintain a continuous study and analysis of the bank's deposit situation in order to properly plan the appropriate utilization of the bank's assets.

It is recognized that variable portions of the bank's assets must be maintained in cash for the purpose of providing:

1. *Till money. (Currency and coin for the purpose of supplying depositors' requirements.)*
2. *Required reserves with The Federal Reserve Bank.*
3. *Balances deposited with other banks as compensa-*

tion for correspondent bank services.

It is obvious that some portion of our cash assets will always be in transit and therefore will not be eligible for use or investment by us until actually received.

It shall be the duty of the comptroller of the bank to determine the extent and amount of cash required for each of the above named purposes. The comptroller shall provide the Conversion Committee a daily statement of the estimated funds required for each of the above described purposes.

The senior lending officer shall inform the Conversion Committee from day to day as to the volume of loans outstanding, commitments for loans to be consummated in the future and scheduled reductions of outstanding loans.

The investment officer shall inform the Conversion Committee from day to day of maturing investments or unfilled orders for the purchase of securities.

The Conversion Committee shall keep the senior executive officers of the bank informed as to the bank's cash and reserve position, and in decisions involving unusually large amounts or matters of policy, the senior executive officers shall be consulted in the deliberations of the Conversion Committee.

After giving due consideration to all of the factors mentioned above, the Conversion Committee on each banking day shall determine whether the bank has any funds which may or should be invested, also the extent to which funds may be needed for reserve requirements, correspondent banks, or till money, or for other purposes.

The Conversion Committee from time to time, as conditions may make it necessary or desirable, shall request the investment officer to purchase Federal funds or liquidate investments for needed purposes, or shall inform the

128

investment officer that funds are available for investment.

The investment officer shall execute such purchases and sales of securities as may seem necessary and desirable to carry out the requests of the Conversion Committee, all such purchases and sales to be in accordance with the provisions of the bank's by-laws, and sales and purchases in unusually large amounts or in unusual situations should be made only after consultation with senior executive officers.

In the selection of securities for bank investment, the following principles and policies shall be observed:

General Investment Standards

1. While commercial banking is a business that necessarily involves some degree of business risks, such risks so far as the employment of funds is concerned, should primarily be limited to loans rather than securities. Security purchases are therefore to be made with primary consideration to safety and liquidity. Security purchases should be limited to prime, short, and medium term securities, representing the ultimate in safety and flexibility. Quality and maturity will not be ignored to obtain yield. Securities for the bank investment account will be purchased in the expectation that they will be held to call or maturity, and not for the purpose of trading or resale.

Secondary Reserve

2. The historical record of the deposits of this bank reveals that there is a wide fluctuation of deposits on both the monthly cycle and the annual cycle. There has frequently been a recurring fluctuation of 10% in total deposits within a 30 day period, and traditionally there has been a seasonal slump of deposits beginning in the early spring and continuing until the end of the summer months.

The deposit fluctuations, together with the fact that we have a considerable volume of public funds and deposits of other banks which may be subject to unexpected withdrawal, suggest that we should maintain a substantial secondary reserve of government securities with maturities not longer than two years. The secondary reserve at the period of peak deposits should not be less than 15% of total deposits.

State and Municipal Securities

3. A great many banks maintain approximately 30% of total assets in U.S. Government securities, and about 10% in other types of securities, including state, municipal, and corporate bonds. For some years this bank has maintained approximately 15% of its deposits in state and municipal securities, and only about 20% in U.S. Government securities. We have not purchased any corporate bonds in recent years.

With the investment opportunities that exist in high grade state and municipal bonds and the facilities that our bank possesses to invest in this type of security, we think it is prudent to take advantage of the tax differential in tax free bonds and keep approximately 15% of our deposits invested in high grade state and municipal securities, the maturities to be spaced in accordance with the schedules hereinafter outlined.

State and municipal bonds of other states may be purchased in appropriate amounts when it appears expedient to do so, but generally speaking, preference will be given to securities of our own state. Any securities of other states shall be allocated to the quota of state and municipal securities.

U.S. Government Securities

4. Approximately 20% to 30% of our deposits should

be invested in U.S. Government securities; depending upon the deposit trend and the resulting size of our secondary reserve.

Industrial Securities

5. Under present conditions, it is not contemplated that we will place any industrial securities in our investmen portfolio.

Maturity Diversification

6. The securities portfolio should be evenly distributed over a relatively short maturity period, allowing a sufficient volume to come due yearly for the purpose of—

(a) Providing adequate cash for abnormal deposit withdrawals when and if necessary; or

(b) For reinvestment during normal deposit requirements.

It will be our objective to restrict our bond maturities to the following maturity schedule:

No maturities beyond	15 years
98% within	10 years
80% within	5 years
60% within	3 years
45% within	2 years
25% within	1 year

The above maturity schedule is intended to represent appropriate diversification of maturity holdings and under some circumstances it may be desirable to have virtually all of our securities in very short term maturities.

The Bank Management Commission of the American Bankers Association has published a booklet entitled "Statement of Principles and Standards of Investment for Commercial Banks," and this publication is well worthy of consideration by any bank in determining its investment policies.

The determination of what portion of a bank's resources are investible, and in what media of investments it should be employed, is sometimes referred to as "the conversion function," that is to say, the conversion of cash into earning assets.

Since the conversion of available, investible funds into earning assets is a commercial bank's principal source of income, the importance of a definite plan in this respect cannot be over-emphasized.

The decision as to what portion of a bank's assets is investible almost necessarily begins with an analysis of not only the existing deposits, but a study of the deposit trends in the past as to various types of deposits and an estimate of future deposit trends, both seasonal for the short term outlook, as well as the longer term future trend.

One of the principal points to be constantly borne in mind in any such analysis of deposits is the possible deposit vulnerability. This must be measured in the light of the possible national deposit pattern, as well as the local approach.

In the national approach consideration must be given to the factors which may be expected to decrease or increase the aggregate bank deposits in the nation. There are at least five factors which historically have served to decrease deposits in the past:

1. A decrease in aggregate loans in the banking system.
2. A decrease in aggregate security holdings.
3. An outflow of gold from the country.
4. An increase in money in circulation.
5. An increase in Federal Reserve Bank credit outstanding.

A contrary movement in any of these five factors would tend to either increase deposits or to diminish deposit declines caused by the other factors. The forecast of aggregate deposits throughout the banking system must take all of these factors into consideration. This information can readily be obtained from the periodical reports of the Federal Reserve System.

In addition to the forecast at the national level, it is necessary to make a local study which will take into consideration the economy of the region and community in which the bank is situated; the nature of the bank's deposits as to public funds; diversification of business or industries; percentage of time deposits; seasonal trends resulting from agriculture; tourist activity or other such factors, as well as the degree to which deposit funds may be concentrated in a few large accounts.

After making a studied estimate of the bank's probable deposit volume with special reference to the lowest probable levels, a similar study and estimate should be made of the probable loan volume for the purpose of forecasting the potential peaks that may become desirable.

Having determined the possible low in deposits, and the probable high in loans, the pattern of reserves can be planned.

The Primary Reserve represents the minimum amount of cash on hand, or "till money" and deposits with banks which should be maintained. It is an extravagant and wasteful policy to keep too large a balance in "till money" and "due from banks." No specific yardsticks exist for determining the exact amount to be kept in the Primary Reserve. Enough cash must at all times be on hand in the bank to meet any reasonable and foreseeable demands and requirements of customers, and sufficient balances must be carried in correspondent banks to reasonably compensate them for services rendered. Within this framework, management must determine the minimum and maximum levels of the Primary Reserve.

For members of the Federal Reserve System, the legal reserve required at "The Fed" is a matter of Federal Reserve Regulations, and must be adhered to. In times of "easy money", bankers are apt to be careless and allow their excess reserves at the Federal Reserve to reach extravagant levels. In times of "tight money" even well managed banks sometimes have difficulty in maintaining their required reserves at the Fed and frequently have to borrow or "buy Federal funds" to meet the semi-monthly required average balances for the legal reserve. Non-member banks should maintain liquid reserves similar to the legal reserves required for members of the Federal Reserve System.

The Secondary Reserve, consisting of liquid securities, is a protection against decreasing deposits and increasing loans. Since the Secondary Reserve represents the volatile portion of the bank's investment assets, it should consist largely of the highest grade short-term securities.

After estimating the Primary and Secondary Reserves, it is then possible to arrive at a theoretical balance available for the bank's investment portfolio. While commercial banking is a business that involves calculated risks, the risks should normally be confined to the loan account rather than included in the investment portfolio. While the investment policies of well managed banks will differ as to the degree of investment risk which they will advisedly undertake and the maturity range, it should be stressed that good banking management insists upon conservatism and high quality in this area.

Capital gains, through profits on the sale of securities,

are not to be considered as normal income in the conduct of a commercial bank and any such profits are usually allocated to special reserve accounts rather than included in normal earnings or carried in undivided profits.

Under certain circumstances, it is distinctly advantageous for banks to sell securities and take a loss for tax purposes. Appropriate procedures should be maintained in every bank so that the possibilities of such sales for tax purposes will be considered periodically.

Although the Loans and Discounts are not included in either the Primary, Legal, or Secondary Reserves of a bank, nor are they technically a part of the bank's investment portfolio, nevertheless, the Loan and Discounts play an important part in the conversion of funds program of a commercial bank, and the head of the Loan and Discount Department should be a member of the Conversion Committee for a number of reasons. First, for the purpose of being intimately familiar with the bank's investible funds situation as a guide to the formulation of lending plans and policies; second, for the purpose of keeping the Conversion Committee informed of loan commitments and outlook; and third, for the purpose of coordinating the possible use of loans and discounts as rediscount loans eligible for rediscount which may constitute a third line of reserves.

In establishing a Conversion Committee in a medium sized bank, the committee should include, in addition to the senior loan officer, mentioned above, the senior investment officer and the Comptroller or senior officer charged with the responsibility of the bank's cash on hand and cash due from and due to other banks. The bank's senior executive might well be included as a member of the Conversion Committee, but the committee should probably not exceed four members. It is desirable that such a committee meet daily for the purpose of reviewing the bank's cash position, its situation with respect to required legal reserves, its loan commitments and its investible position.

In planning an investment program for the employment of the funds of a commercial bank, it is likely that it will not consist of a single program, but rather a group of formulas or plans that should be coordinated into an overall plan.

While it may not be expedient or desirable to definitely allocate investment purchases to the various types of deposit funds, the difference in the several types of deposit funds should definitely influence the investment pattern.

The analysis of the bank's various classes of deposits will determine, to a large extent, the pattern of the investment program.

The source of the funds to be invested should influence the type and maturity of the investments to be selected. For instance, regular demand deposits, "due to banks" funds, public funds, savings deposits, and time certificates might each be treated in a somewhat different manner.

In addition to the analysis of the deposits, the bank's capital accounts should also be analyzed to determine what portion, if any, of the capital funds are available for conversion or investment. For instance, some banks may have all of the capital funds invested in a bank building and the capital funds available for investment might even be negative, which would have the effect of reducing the other funds available for investment.

An analysis of the capital accounts and the various types of deposits will permit the Conversion Committee to set up a desired balance sheet by percentages resulting from the theoretical investment policies determined upon. In parallel columns should be inserted the actual balance sheet percentages for each item in both assets and liabilities. The comparative columns will indicate the nature of the investment action needed to bring the bank's investment position in line with the policies and desired investment position of the bank.

For more detailed information as to how deposit sources may be analyzed and formulas established for the various types of reserves and investment accounts, the following books are recommended:

YOUR BANK, ITS DEPOSITS AND ITS INVESTMENTS. Published by The First National Bank of Boston, Mass.

CONVERSION OF COMMERCIAL BANK FUNDS. By Harold E. Zarker. Published by Bankers Publishing Company of Boston, Mass.

Another helpful text on bank investments is:

THE MANAGEMENT OF BANK FUNDS. By Roland I. Robinson. Published by McGraw-Hill Book Company, Inc.

CHAPTER XI

Banking Operations

As HAS BEEN FREQUENTLY OBSERVED, there is a considerable lack of uniformity among banks as to terminology, titles, and organizational setup. If the executive heads of ten different banks were asked to define the term "banking operations," and to describe the functions it embraces, it is almost certain that a wide diversity of answers would be received.

If this is true, it is desirable to define the term "banking operations" so that at least for the purposes of this text, there will be no doubt as to the banking functions that are to be considered under this head.

For this purpose, banking operations might be defined as "the physical handling of money, written instruments representing money (such as checks, drafts and notes), and the preparation and maintenance of accounting records of depositors' accounts." By way of illustration, this definition would include the following banking functions: paying and receiving tellers, proof, transit, individual ledger bookkeeping, analysis, service charges, and statements. Banking functions that definitely would not be included in banking operations would include lending, (although the loan tellers and loan records are normally included) audit, investments and trust business.

There are certain other departments which, in some banks, might be supervised by the banking operations officers, although they are not strictly speaking, banking functions, and in many banks would not be considered as a part of banking operations. Examples of such departments are:—general accounting, safe deposit, personnel administration, and general operations (such as mail, telephone operators, purchasing, guards, building operations and maintenance.)

Sometimes it has been said that the people engaged in banking operations are "the forgotten men of banking". This idea, no doubt, arises from the fact that frequently promotion is slower and pay scales lower than in some other phases of banking. This situation has been discussed to some extent in Chapter V under the subject of job evaluation.

There is no specific education or training which will teach the intricacies of many phases of bank operations other than "on the job" training. It therefore takes time and experience to learn many of these jobs and there appear to be no short cuts. However, since no technical skills or formal education are a prerequisite to operating jobs, there always seems to be a liberal supply of beginners who are willing to undertake such jobs. Percentagewise, a larger number of unskilled bank employees are engaged in banking operations than in any other phase of banking. This factor of a large number of available people may have some bearing on the pay scale of banking operation departments, as contrasted with some of the departments where there are fewer people involved and experienced workers are, therefore, scarcer.

Some other departments, such as investments, credit analysis, general accounting, etc., involve requirements that make both a broad general education and technical training desirable. Supply and demand is a factor that cannot be ignored in job pricing and undoubtedly has an important bearing in determining the salary evaluation of a particular job.

Although it appears to be one of the facts of banking that operation jobs are not as high in salary evaluation as some of the more technical functions, nevertheless, the operating functions are tremendously important insofar as the bank's efficiency and reputation are concerned. A bank's record for accuracy must be good if it is to prosper and enjoy a good reputation. A bank with a weak bookkeeping department or inefficient, careless tellers cannot be expected to merit customer satisfaction, which is the only sound basis for growth.

It can be truthfully said without exaggeration that banking operations constitute the very heart of commercial banking.

It is not intended that this text should provide a detailed treatise on how banking operations are conducted. At most, it is desired to give a resume of sound philosophy and proper attitude of management with respect to this phase of banking. Among the functions that will be discussed somewhat in detail are:— tellers, bookkeeping, transit, proof, and general accounting.

The remainder of this chapter is devoted to a discussion of some of the phases of banking operations with particular reference to some of the current questions of procedures and equipment concerned in such functions.

TELLERS

One of the questions of procedure that frequently arises as to tellers is, whether tellers should be specialized as to paying only, or receiving only, or whether the same teller should handle both the receipt of deposits and the cashing of checks. Another question that arises in medium sized and large banks with respect to tellers is whether each teller shall restrict his activities to an alphabetical segment of customers (such as A-F, G-K, etc.) or whether any customer may go to any teller without regard to the initials of the customer.

Local conditions will necessarily control decisions as to whether bank tellers will handle both deposits and paying, and whether accounts will be grouped alphabetically by tellers. Unquestionably, combination paying and receiving tellers, and no grouping of accounts alphabetically, results in greater flexibility and is more desirable from the customers' viewpoint, but in larger banks it presents a number of operating difficulties. For instance, there is a limit to the number of customers and signatures that a teller can reasonably be expected to be familiar with or have accessible. Unless the accounts are grouped alphabetically, it is impracticable for the tellers to look up signature cards, yet there is more reason to expect that they will need to look up signatures more frequently.

The paying function is more difficult than the receiving function, since the latter does not involve the instant decision to pay or not to pay that confronts a paying teller on nearly every transaction. For this reason, new tellers are frequently well trained as receiving tellers before they are permitted to pay checks.

Receiving deposits is normally a slower process than cashing checks, and when the functions are separated, sometimes receiving tellers' lines are crowded while the paying tellers are idle. When the same teller both pays and receives, it tends to balance the lines. Such a system also removes the necessity for a customer's going to two different windows and perhaps standing in line twice. Bank management should study carefully the local situation and consider all of the arguments pro and con concerning the tellers' system and reach a decision as to what seems most desirable and expedient under the local circumstances.

The equipment of bank tellers has been fairly well standardized in recent years to improve the efficiency of tellers' operations. A teller should have easy access to the signature files and either direct oral or telephone communication with the individual account bookkeepers. A coin dispensing machine expedites the disbursing of coins and also is an aid in accuracy.

At least two manufacturers have highly satisfactory teller's machines which make a permanent record of all transactions and issue printed receipts for deposits. The equipment dealers claim that teller's machines speed up a teller's operation by 20%. While this will probably not always be true, the use of teller's machines does result in a faster operation and also makes possible tighter audit control over tellers' operations.

The use of pre-packaged currency in convenient denominations and amounts speeds up the operation of a paying teller's window. However, the labor involved in the pre-packaging process sometimes proves a problem.

In an attempt to speed up the service at tellers' windows and avoid customers waiting in line, some banks have arranged special tellers' windows which handle certain types of business exclusively, thereby removing such transactions from the regular tellers.

Such a practice that has proven popular is to have certain tellers designated to handle the preparation and delivery of payrolls. The information needed for the preparation of payrolls is usually delivered twenty-four hours in advance.

Such "special tellers' windows" include the handling of certain large business accounts which have large amounts of coin for deposit, such as a bus company, the telephone company, bottled beverage companies, etc. Such a special teller would handle only a few customers each day, but each such deposit would require a considerable time to handle. Sometimes such customers, who deposit daily, are assigned a definite time schedule each day so that they will not have to wait, and at the same time, will not cause other customers to wait while such a wholesale deposit is being verified.

Banking by mail, "Rush hour" depositories, and twenty-four hour depositories are also methods of avoiding waiting in line at tellers' windows.

Some banks that have combination "Paying and Receiving Tellers" have one or more "Paying Only" tellers where the line of customers can be expected to move faster since it will not be slowed up by deposits which are somewhat slower to handle.

The average commercial bank has more personal contacts with its customers through the tellers than at any other point in the bank, and the importance of courteous, quick, and accurate teller's service cannot be over-emphasized.

INDIVIDUAL LEDGER BOOKKEEPING

While the bookkeeping machine operators do not usually have direct personal contact with customers, accurate records with respect to depositors' accounts can make a tremendous difference in a bank's public relations.

The public assumes, as a matter of course, that a bank's bookkeeping will be absolutely accurate, and while a bank will seldom receive praise for bookkeeping accuracy, an occasional mistake will produce intense dissatisfaction. Cross entries, failure to check signatures and endorsements, ignoring stop payment orders, and mistakes of that nature, will cause a lack of confidence on the part of customers that is hard to overcome, to say nothing of the potential liability involved.

Individual ledger bookkeeping in commercial banks is fairly well standardized, although there are several different types of bookkeeping machines and systems, all of which are good.

The question of single posting or double posting and whether to use delayed posting can be effectively debated on both sides since there are very valid arguments pro and con. As with many operational procedures, the decision as to the most appropriate system in a particular bank must be decided on the local situation. What is best and most expedient in one bank may be entirely impractical for another bank in the same city.

It is an elementary policy in commercial banking that any and all information concerning a customer's financial affairs must be treated as strictly confidential by all bank personnel. This principle must constantly be kept in mind in the bookkeeping department where the employees have constant access to the depositors' balances, checks, and deposits. Most banks decline to give information concerning customers' balances over the telephone since it is often difficult to identify the customer's voice. Any such requests to the bookkeeping department are normally referred to an officer, who will use his discretion in giving the requested information or in explaining to the customer that for the customer's protection, such information should not be given by telephone. For similar reasons, it is not good practice to accept stop payment orders by telephone.

PROOF DEPARTMENT

The verification and distribution of customers' deposits is a function that must be performed by every commercial bank however large or small. The manner in which this procedure is performed and the equipment that is used varies widely, according to the size of the bank. Unquestionably there are many different systems or methods which are efficient and acceptable under certain conditions and circumstances. Sometimes a system and equipment which has been perfectly satisfactory for handling the proof function in a given bank for a long period, may become obsolete and inefficient when the bank grows and expands.

In adopting a proof system, it is wise to set up a system that will permit normal growth and expansion without a radical change in the system.

A number of different proof systems are described in the A.I.B. textbook entitled "Principles of Bank Operation". Bank operating officers should be familiar with each of these types of proof systems, and the equipment involved and then adopt such system and equipment as seems to best fit the local situation.

A fundamental principle to bear in mind in connection with a proof system is that all debits and credits from all departments should flow through the proof department, thereby proving the entire bank.

TRANSIT

The transit department takes on special significance when a bank seeks deposits from other banks, since the collecting of checks on out-of-town banks is one of the principal services that a bank can perform for its correspondent bank depositors.

There is sometimes a conflict of interest between the bank operations officers and the bank relations officers as to policy in routing transit items. The bank relations men usually want to establish as many direct sending points as possible, as a selling argument in getting correspondent bank deposits. The operating officers on the other hand, usually tend to restrict the number of direct sending points for the purpose of efficiency and economy.

Since the inauguration of the Federal Reserve System, the collection and clearing of out-of-town checks has been greatly simplified, and a large portion of the checks on Federal Reserve Member Banks are cleared through the Federal Reserve System.

The collection of checks on non-member banks is usually accomplished through forwarding such items to the correspondent bank nearest the drawee bank, and any bank soliciting deposits and transit items from other banks, therefore, should be in a position to forward such non-par items to a bank not too far distant from the drawee bank. Such a system requires the forwarding bank to maintain deposits with correspondent banks over a wide area, and can immobilize funds that might otherwise be profitably employed.

Since banks seek deposits for the purpose of making a profit from them, the indirect as well as the direct cost of handling transit items should be considered for cost accounting purposes.

Most large city banks and some other banks which specialize in correspondent bank accounts, operate an "around the clock" transit service to speed up the check collecting service, but comparatively few medium sized banks have found that night transit service is needed by their customers or that the benefits will justify the additional expense required.

In determining the appropriate number of direct sending points, a "middle of the road" policy is suggested, with the average volume of items in any given locality being the determining factor.

GENERAL ACCOUNTING

As stated above, general accounting may not be strictly classified as banking operations, since accounting of this type is common to all business enterprises in some degree, but it is frequently supervised by the same officer personnel as banking operations. In addition to the routine and required functions in the general accounting of the bank, this department can be of inestimable value to the management of a bank by providing records and statistics that will enable management to fully comprehend all phases of the bank's operations and to intelligently plan for the future.

Records, reports, and statistics have but little value unless they are fully understood, correctly interpreted, and used. Not only the top executive officers, but the Board of Directors as well, should be provided with periodical reports from the general accounting department that will clearly reflect what is currently happening in the bank and the trends that can be discerned by comparative figures for other periods.

The most logical time for such statistical reviews is the monthly meeting of the Board of Directors. Instead of giving such monthly statistical reports orally to the Board, many banks provide each director with a ring binder book in which is placed each month the detailed reports concerning each department of the bank for the preceding month, the year to date, and for comparative periods in the preceding year. This data is usually prepared by the general accounting department.

The general accounting records of a bank should be maintained in such condition that the department can at any time, on short notice, provide the management with almost any type of statistical information concerning the bank's operations that the executive officers or directors may desire.

ACCEPTING NEW DEPOSIT ACCOUNTS

One of the important functions in banking operations is the procedure followed in opening depositors' accounts. The opening of a deposit account is a matter of a contract agreement between the customer and the bank, and is usually handled by some one of officer level representing the bank.

While banks are always interested in obtaining desirable new deposit accounts, it should be borne in mind that there are certain potential liabilities in connection with every deposit account and banks should use due care in opening new accounts. A bank is not obligated to open an account for any person who applies, and it has the right to decline any account which does not appear to be desirable.

It is understandable that policies in accepting new accounts will be different in various banks. To mention two extremes, some large metropolitan banks are not interested in accepting checking accounts from individuals where the initial deposit is less than $1,000, while in small banks such accounts are the prevailing type.

There are numerous ways in which a bank account

can be used to defraud both the depository bank and the public, and a bank should be reasonably satisfied that the depositor is a person of good reputation who does not intend to use the account for wrongful or questionable purposes. A checking account which frequently has checks issued against insufficient balances is objectionable to banks and such accounts are to be avoided rather than sought.

Some banks make a practice of conducting an investigation before accepting new accounts, but while in theory this would be desirable, in most small and medium sized banks it is likely to be impracticable unless the practice is more or less uniform in all of the local banks. In any event, the person opening the new account should obtain positive identification of the new depositor and be reasonably satisfied from the depositor's address, occupation, and references, that it is a bona fide deposit.

Accepting a new account from a stranger and receiving an out of town check for immediate credit in such an account is a dangerous procedure which will often result in trouble. The individuals charged with the responsibility of opening new accounts should be experienced bankers who are thoroughly aware of the possibilities of fraud. While it is important to be cordial and gracious in dealing with prospective new customers, the bank's new account representatives must constantly bear in mind that accounts must be received on a selective basis and not be so eager for additional new business that care and discretion are not exercised.

ACCOUNT ANALYSIS AND SERVICE CHARGES

The practice of banks' making service charges on checking accounts based on balances and activity, is now followed in all but the very small banks. The fairness of such charges has become universally recognized as the custom and practice has spread.

There is a lack of uniformity among banks throughout the country as to the methods and rates used in computing service charges, and this is to be expected and probably will always be true. Service charges, to be on a sound basis, should be founded on accurate cost accounting figures computed on a local basis.

It is usually impracticable to undertake detailed account analysis on small accounts for the reason that the probable cost of such analyses might equal or exceed the service charges. For this reason, on small accounts, and non-business accounts, a partial analysis, or a simplified system of "metered service charges" is often employed.

Theoretically, it would be equitable and fair if both the service charges and allowance for investible balances could be varied from month to month as costs and investment income fluctuate, however, frequent variations or adjustments in service charges would be productive of such confusion that it is impracticable. At reasonable intervals, however, it is desirable to take a fresh look at the service charge scale to see if it is obsolete on either the charge or credit side, and it is only reasonable that readjustments will have to be made from time to time.

When service charges first became popular some years ago, it was the custom for all local banks in the same community to enter into an agreement fixing uniform service charges. Subsequently, court decisions have ruled that such agreements are "in restraint of trade," and therefore illegal. It is apparently not illegal for banks to levy uniform charges, however, if there is no agreement to that effect.

The American Bankers Association has published a very practical and useful manual discussing and describing systems of service charges for small banks and any bank that has not adopted a system of such charges should give consideration to the recommendations contained in the said manual.

Despite the widespread use of account analysis and service charges by commercial banks, there is still a need for further customer education on the subject. This is an important phase of bank public relations and should not be neglected.

STATEMENTS

One of the principal contacts which a commercial bank has with many checking account customers is through the depositor's statement. To a depositor who lives out of town and seldom comes to the bank, the statement may be his only contact over extended periods of time.

Perhaps the primary consideration of a bank statement is accuracy. Unless it is absolutely accurate, it has no value and is certain to be productive of confusion and trouble. Following closely behind the requirement of accuracy should be legibility and neatness. Smudges, erasures, and cross entries should not be permitted on bank statements.

Any bank bookkeeping system that does not produce accurate, legible, neat statements is less than satisfactory.

In the past, it was customary for most banks to render nearly all checking account customers a monthly statement with cancelled checks as of the end of each calendar month. In a sizable bank the preparation of monthly statements on all checking accounts on any particular date, is a herculean task that requires the services of practically all available employees. In banks where this practice is still followed, "statement night" is an occasion to be dreaded. The shifting of employees from their normal duties to the preparation of statements once a month is frequently the occasion of personnel friction and complications.

To avoid the disagreeable features of "statement night" most large and medium sized banks have adopted a staggered system of statements so that some statements are prepared each business day instead of all being handled at the end of the calendar month.

This system of staggered statement dates has been almost universally adopted by public utility companies and many department stores. Banks adopting it have not met with much customer resistance, although it is usually necessary to schedule statements of business accounts on the last day of the month rather than an interim date.

COLLECTION DEPARTMENT

The principal service rendered by a bank collection department is the presentment and collection of drafts and other financial instruments that cannot be handled through bank clearings and transit letters. Such instruments usually require individual handling rather than in batches, as in the case of cash items.

A problem that frequently arises is the desire of customers to handle drafts and other such instruments as cash items for immediate credit rather than as collection items for credit when collection is effected. From the bank's viewpoint, it is much safer and more expedient to handle such items through the collection department rather than as cash items for immediate credit. One of the principal advantages of handling an item through the collection department rather than transit is that it can provide affirmative notice of payment or other special handling when desirable.

The individual handling of items and the cost of messenger service and postal service increases the handling costs of such items considerably beyond the cost of cash items. The rather nominal charges usually made for collection items reduces the possibility of any profits from this type of business.

SAVINGS DEPARTMENT

When a savings department is maintained in a commercial bank there are usually three reasons:— (1) the encouragement of thrift in the community; (2) the supplying of a needed service to customers in the hope of retaining customers and attracting customers for other departments; and (3) making a profit through the operation of the savings department.

Sometimes the profit motive is minimized or overlooked and the savings department is regarded as a public service or necessary nuisance, with but little or no profit possibilities.

The fact that many savings banks are profitably operated without any commercial bank activities should be ample evidence that a savings department may be a profitable venture if it has proper management.

Since there are several different phases of the management of a savings department, namely: operations, investment, promotion, etc., management should determine whether all phases are to be coordinated through a savings manager, or whether the various functions are to be supervised by the department heads who direct such activities in the other parts of the bank.

There is much to be said for the policy of having some one individual of officer rank plan, coordinate, and give immediate supervision to the various functions of the department. Without this type of supervision some of the phases of the savings department are apt to be neglected without top management being aware of it.

The officers in charge of banking operations should make it their responsibility to keep informed of the various systems and procedures followed in other banks, as well as the various types of equipment that are available to perform the various jobs, and then decide what is best under the particular circumstances under which they are operating.

The National Association of Bank Auditors and Comptrollers, through its local, regional, and national meetings, and its various publications, including "Auditgrams", is one of the best means of bank operations personnel keeping abreast of developments in this field.

While it is seldom desirable to make changes in systems and procedure just to try something new, bank operating men should not be lacking in courage to adopt new methods, procedures, systems, or machines when, after careful study, it seems justified.

CHAPTER XII

Automation in Bank Accounting

AUTOMATION IS A GENERAL TERM which is used in many ways. It is defined in Webster's Unabridged Dictionary as "a system or method in which many or all of the processes are automatically performed or controlled by machinery or electronic devices."

In a manufacturing plant automation may be used widely to control machines that formerly were manually controlled by persons. Automation in manufacturing processes, however, is quite different from what we call automation in bank accounting, although both are frequently controlled by electronic devices.

In bank accounting, automation is usually by means of electronic data processing and in most systems is accomplished through punched cards, punched tape, magnetic tape, or electro-magnetic character recognition.

Magnetic ink character recognition (usually referred to by the initials MICR) is perhaps the latest development in automation insofar as bank accounting is concerned, and is largely responsible for the tremendous increase in automation in bank accounting in recent years.

Electronic data processing (or EDP) is a term that to some extent has replaced the word "automation" as a general term in referring to automatic accounting for banks.

The tremendous increase of interest in and use of automation in bank accounting in recent years is the result of a number of factors:

1.   The increased use of banking by the so-called "little man." Retail banking, in the narrow sense, has resulted in many checking accounts with low average balances and in a disproportionate number of deposits and checks for small amounts. This has resulted in increasing the volatility factor, or to express it another way, more items to process per dollar of deposits.

Since the item count in most banks has been increasing faster than deposit growth, the bank must handle more items without proportionate increased deposits to compensate for such additional items.

2.   Another factor that has served to increase banks' item costs is the steady increase in clerical salaries resulting from mininmum wage laws and other economic factors. It is simply getting too expensive to pay prevailing clerical wage rates for such routine functions as the manual processing of checks and deposits. As wages have increased employee productivity has not increased accordingly and this has of course resulted in costing more dollars to handle the same number of items. In a limited degree, bank clerical labor is pricing itself out of a market.

3.   There is a limit to the extent that bank service charges can be increased to keep up with the increasing cost of handling items. At some place there is a point of diminishing return and increased service charges will result in fewer customers and proportionately smaller income.

4.   Other economic factors such as shrinking balances,

higher rates on savings deposits, increased costs of supplies, equipment, and occupancy costs of banking rooms are also tending to increase banking costs and make it necessary for the banker to cut his costs to protect his prices and his market.

Projecting the rate of item increase in recent years into the future, and taking into consideration the trend toward higher costs per item it has become very apparent that banks must find methods for handling the mounting volume of routine paper processing in faster and cheaper ways. Electronic data processing seems to offer the best solution to this problem.

All of the above reasons may be summarized in the simple statement that electronic data processing in bank accounting, is to a large extent, a defensive move to halt the steady rise in bank costs.

In addition to the possibility of reducing item costs, some of the other advantages which might be obtained by using electronic data processing equipment in banking operations may be listed as follows:

1.   Much faster posting and the elimination of deferred posting, thereby permitting all acounts to be properly posted and balanced before the beginning of each banking day.

2.   The automatic calculation and posting of service charges.

3.   The handling of an increased number of items through growth without requiring a proportionate increase in personnel or equipment.

4.   The minimizing of the possibility of cross entries between accounts on deposits and checks.

5.   Provide better control on the payment of uncollected funds.

6. The preparation of transit letters and clearing items in local banks automatically as a by-product of sorting and listing.

7. Providing automatic control of overdrafts at predetermined levels.

8. Providing better statistical control for management.

9. The providing of additional new services to customers such as one-check payroll credits, and other external applications.

10. Providing EDP service for smaller correspondent banks.

Other possible objectives that might be attained are:

1. With a computer system with random access storage, a central information file may be automatically maintained on every customer of the bank which will instantaneously show the following: A daily statement of the total amount of money on deposit, both demand and savings; amount of money owed to bank by type of loan, how credit has been handled, paying record, credit line, the officer who handled the loans, and other such information that management needs to give better and faster service to customers.

2. Management reports may be maintained on each loan officer showing:

a. New loans made—amount and type.

b. Collection record—amount of loans past due, interest past due.

c. Periodical reports on loans due to be paid; also amount of interest due to be collected. With this information, management is in a better position to consider investment plans, or consider applications for new loans.

3.   All savings accounts may have interest computed daily. Day-by-day interest requirements for the six-month period may be obtained.

4.   As account balances change in the demand deposit accounts, a daily report on any increase or decrease over a stated amount may be provided. This will give a daily follow up for a personal call by a bank officer if it is deemed desirable.

Other, indirect advantages which might be obtained are:

1.   A decreased number of personnel which should reduce the turnover rate, thereby reducing the cost of orienting and training new employees, which cost is considerable.

2.   A reduction in the number of supervisory personnel required.

3.   A reduction in the aggregate cost of fringe benefits as a result of employing fewer people.

4.   The faster service and prestige which should result from using the most modern accounting methods.

There are also significant advantages to be obtained in departments other than demand deposit accounting, such as the storage, computing and printing of income tax data in the Trust Department and in the General Accounting Department, the computing of daily interest in the Savings Department, the compiling and billing of the late charges in the Installment Loan Department.

There are many different degrees and systems of bank automation. Many such systems that were thought quite modern and advanced a few years ago would be considered obsolete today.

All of the principal manufacturers of data processing equipment collaborated with the American Bankers Association in establishing a uniform system of magnetic ink character recognition symbols. MICR is a common language which both humans and electronic equipment can easily read. The magnetic ink used in MICR symbols contains a metallic substance which will operate electronic devices in EDP equipment. The standardization of the symbols as to character size and placement on items makes it possible for items to be processed interchangeably between banks using equipment of different manufacturers.

The Federal Reserve System, in recognition of the growing acceptance of bank automation and the need to standardize such procedures so as to simplify bank examinations and aid in the assembling, comparison, and interpretation of data, has promulgated a system of account classification that will aid in this purpose. The Federal Reserve System is also encouraging all banks to use MICR transit numbers on all checks to aid in the processing and sorting of checks in transit.

The fact that the Federal Reserve Banks which are heavy users of electronic data processing equipment have deemed it expedient to make plans and issue instructions to member banks with respect to automation, is strong evidence that such accounting procedures have met with full acceptance and are here to stay.

There is no standardized or uniform system of bank accounting by automation. Even one manufacturer might have several different systems, offering different degrees of automation and different abilities and capacities.

The equipment of data processing systems can be classified as to purpose as follows:

1. *Input*

    Input may be by means of MICR, punched cards, punched tape, magnetic tape, plus manual input.

2. *Storage*

Storage may be accomplished through punched cards, tape, or magnetic discs, drums or cores. Storage is like an electronic filing system, completely indexed and instantaneously accessible.

3. *Processing*

The central processing unit is usually designated as a computer. The central processing unit controls and supervises the entire electronic data processing system and performs the actual arithmetic and logical operations on data. Functionally, the computer has two sections—control and arithmetic-logical.

The control section directs and coordinates all operations called for by the instructions contained in the program. In some ways the control section is like a telephone exchange which connects all of the units included in the EDP system. The control section can start or stop a unit, turn signals off or on, or direct some process of calculation.

The arithmetic-logical section contains the devices to perform calculating and logical operations. The logical portion executes the decision making operations to change the sequence of program execution.

It is to be observed that while a computer is capable of performing many remarkable operations, it cannot *think*, and it can only return in output, data that has been previously received as input, although the form, nature and sequence of the data may have been rearranged.

4. *Output*

The output in most systems is through the medium

of a high speed printer, punched cards, punched tape or magnetic tape.

All systems of bank automation do not include computers and printers. Some banks use punched cards for input, sorting and storage, without the computer application, and without a high speed printer.

Some banks use electronic devices to sort and list items that are posted manually.

A typical electronic data processing system in a bank might include the following equipment:

1.   A sorter reader which will handle intermixed checks, deposit slips or other random-sized documents, and sort them into any desired groupings or sequence. As the documents pass through the sorter reader, the magnetic inscribed characters on the documents may be listed, accumulated, stored, or printed as desired.

2.   Several proof inscribers for printing magnetic ink characters on checks, deposit slips, or other documents. Such a machine while inscribing documents will also provide detailed lists with totals for each control classification, also a detailed master tape covering all items included in the batch, and it will automatically print an endorsement on the back of each check. Encoders without the listing and accumulation features may be used for encoding only where listing is not required and such machines are usually cheaper than proof inscribers which may perform several other functions.

3.   A card read punch machine which will punch cards for any desired code, read and interpret punched cards, check the data on cards punched, or read and stack the cards in the sequence and classification desired.

4.   A processing unit or computer which can utilize as input MICR documents, magnetic tape or punched

cards, and provides inter-system communication with other units through interchangeability of tape. Such a computer will accept data and instructions of variable length and will store data and programs. Such a computer will add, subtract, multiply, and divide. It will also make automatic comparison of data, and will store the data for future utilization.

5.   Reports from a computer will usually be accomplished through a high speed printer which may be connected on line with the computer and will print the computer output at the rate of approximately 600 lines per minute.

6.   The storage of data is frequently accomplished through magnetic tape units which are connected on line with the computer. Both the input and output are automatic. A medium-sized bank might require from four to six magnetic tape units.

Other miscellaneous equipment which might be required in such an EDP system would be collators for punched cards and key punches.

Electronic data processing equipment may be either bought outright, or leased. Most banks, on account of the high purchase price of such equipment and the possibility of obsolescence through technological improvements prefer to lease instead of purchase. Most such agreements provide for the substitution of improved equipment or later models, at the option of the lessee.

Some banks have refrained from installing electronic data processing equipment because of the many improvements that have been made on the equipment each year in recent years. Such reasoning might lead one not to buy an automobile until the manufacturers quit making improvements on new automobiles.

The choice of an electronic data processing system for a given bank is not an easy task. The bank management must have in mind definite objectives sought to be accomplished. An automation program should not be entered into merely in an attempt to "keep up with the Joneses."

In approaching the problems and opportunities in bank automation for a particular bank, the areas for study can be broken into at least two groupings. In general, the potential applications can be classified as "Internal Automation Applications" and "External Applications." The terms "internal" and "external" in this sense are intended to refer to accounting operations for the bank's own records which are classified as internal, and possibly new accounting services that might be related to customers through automation equipment and that the said equipment would, therefore, be available to take on an additional workload of outside, or external, accounting service which banks are not prepared to handle under old methods, procedures, and equipment.

Before any external accounting work is sought, the bank should fully solve its own internal accounting requirements, including thorough familiarization with the automation equipment and procedures by the bank's personnel.

As to the bank's internal use of automation, it appears that the most significant advantages are directly related to deposit functions, and include sorting, listing, proof, distribution, updating of customers' individual ledgers, and preparation of customers' statements.

Other operations where significant cost reduction opportunities and service improvements might be expected within the bank are: Installment Loan accounting, Savings Department accounting, Trust and Investment accounting,

General accounting, Auditing, Charge Account Service records, and Check-Credit accounting.

If automation is fully installed and the bank's own internal accounting procedures are satisfactorily established, and it appears that an additional workload could be carried by the automation equipment, market research should be undertaken to determine the potential for any other services which might be rendered for customers by the bank with its automation equipment. Such research would involve the collection of statistics as to the specific services that might be sold and the extent of the market that might be reached, and the possible volume of such transactions. The major portion of this research would be actual interviews with potential customers, observation of their paper work operations, and analysis of how readily these operations could be standardized for adaptation to centralized uniform processing. The market research study should provide specific answers to the following questions:

1. What is the total potential market for the bank in rendering external automation service to customers?

2. What service charges would be required by the bank from customers to justify the suggested new services and yield a reasonable profit to the bank?

3. What amount of this potential is immediately and easily obtainable?

4. What amount of such additional new accounting business could likely be obtained through an intensive selling program?

Some of the variables that should influence the choice of an electronic data processing system by a particular bank are—the number of checking accounts, the number of special checking accounts, the number of savings accounts, the total volume of items, the number and distance of any branches, the volume of installment loans and real estate mortgage loans, and the volume of trust accounting, if there is a trust department. A system that might be perfectly appropriate for one bank might not be suitable at all for another bank of approximately equal size, which has a different makeup in the type of business it handles.

The machines and equipment used in electronic data processing are known in the business machine equipment trade as "hardware." The maintenance, service, training, and educational services and other aids furnished by the manufacturer to the user are sometimes referred to as "software."

It is very well established that the "hardware" of all of the larger manufacturers of electronic data processing equipment is workable, practicable, and reasonably efficient. Assuming that appropriate "hardware" is prescribed to fulfill the needs of a given bank, the "software" or service provided by the supplier is just as important or perhaps more important than the "hardware."

For the bank (or banker) which does not have the personnel available or the willingness to perform its own research in the automation field to determine its needs and how they may best be fulfilled, there are a number of well qualified, independent consultants who for reasonable fees will study a bank's situation and recommend what system and equipment will best meet its requirements.

After a bank has decided upon what type of automation system it will install and has placed the order, there is a great deal that must be done before the equipment is received. The installation of an electronic data processing system requires a comprehensive plan of training and education of the bank staff and an extensive program of informing and educating the customers. Selecting and preparing the site for the data processing center is also a project that will require considerable study and time.

Practically all systems of bank automation require the serial numbering of customer accounts. This in itself is quite a burdensome task. There are several systems of account numbering that are commonly used. Straight numerics seems to be the numbering system most frequently used although there are sound arguments in favor of alphanumerics, block numerics, and other systems. The equipment manufacturers do not seem to favor any particular numbering system over the others.

Since the purchase or lease of an electronic data processing system is a sizable contract, and the manufacturer has a definite selfish interest in making certain that the system operates successfully, all of the manufacturers provide banks with considerable help in installing such systems. The "software" includes training employees in all phases of programming and operation. In the larger installations the manufacutrer usually assigns one or more of his representatives to the bank on a full-time basis during the programming and installation period.

The installation of such a system should be a team effort with the co-ordinated participation of a group of the bank staff. It is highly important that an executive be designated as project director and assigned primary responsibility for installing the system and making it work.

The project director should organize a bank staff committee with various members assigned to the several phases of the project such as employee information and training, customer relations and advertising, data processing center, programming, operations, etc.

Perhaps the greatest saving in manpower to be achieved through automation in banks is in the demand deposit function. Some banks begin an automation program by tackling the demand deposit function first and then spread automation to other bank functions such as installment loan accounting, savings accounting, trust operations, investment records, general books, etc. However, since the demand deposit function is perhaps the most complicated of all the departments to be automated, and involves the numbering of the customers' accounts and the processing of a heavy volume of items daily, many banks prefer to begin the automation program in such departments as installment loans or the trust department, and postpone converting demand deposit accounting untill all other departments have been converted and are operating satisfactorily. However, since other departments, such as Installment Loans and Trusts, in many banks depend on punched cards or punched tape for input rather than MICR, experience gained in operating these departments with automation is not particularly helpful in preparing for the handling of demand deposits, which is basically an MICR operation.

The project director should prepare an installation schedule with a target date for each step to be accomplished until the entire program is completely installed. A progress chart should be maintained to indicate whether the installation schedule is lagging.

The question is sometimes asked, "How big must a bank be to justify the installation of automation equipment?" There can no precise answer to such a question. In the first place the word "automation" is such a general term it can mean almost any degree of automatic accounting. The use of full scale electronic data processing equipment, including a computer, is obviously limited to the larger banks, but there are many automatic accounting devices other than computers which may be profitably employed by smaller banks.

Any processing of papers or documents that can be accomplished faster and cheaper by mechanical or electronic equipment is a means of automation that can be profitably used by banks.

The diagnosis for a particular bank must be a tailor-made plan prescribed only after a detailed study of the operations and costs of the bank involved. All of the principal business machine manufacturers will undertake such a study for a bank without any cost or obligation, but the bank management should remember that the purpose of such a survey by a manufacturer is to sell equipment, and any such survey and recommendations by a supplier must be subjected to the closest scrutiny by the banker. If the banker has difficulty in reaching a decision as to whether or not to embark upon an automation program, or which system to adopt, the services of an experienced, independent consultant in this field are needed.

The ultimate success of an automation program for demand deposit accounting involving the use of MICR numbered accounts, inevitably depends upon customer cooperation. The percentage of unqualified items (checks or deposit slips that are not inscribed with the depositor's number in magnetic ink), must be held to a minimum of five per cent or less if the full benefits of automation are to be achieved.

The cooperation and participation of customers will not result automatically from the installation of electronic equipment and such a system. A high percentage of pre-qualified items will be achieved only through a carefully

171

planned program of information and education, both of the bank staff and the customers, and even with a good educational program it will require months of persistent and patient effort.

The information program must be begun internally with the bank staff. Unless all the employees thoroughly understand the program and are sold on it, it will be very difficult to obtain customer understanding and cooperation.

It must be recognized by bankers that the principal advantages of automation in banking are for the bank and not for the customer, although a good system should result in faster service, with fewer errors, and should serve to minimize the possibility of increased service charge rates.

All possible media for disseminating information on automation to both employees and customers should be utilized, including seminars or group meetings, direct mail, newspaper display, newspaper news items, booklets and folders sent with depositors' statements, radio, television, and any other means that might be available.

What are the possibilities of a bank's saving money by reducing expenses through an automation program? This also is a question that is difficult to answer. Theoretically, a good system properly operated should result in lower costs per item, however, there are a number of factors that will operate to minimize any real reduction of expenses in the early part of the operation of a new automation system.

Among such factors are the increased cost of providing new magnetically inscribed checks to depositors, the cost of constructing and equipping a data processing center, the period of parallel operation of the old system and the new system prior to the final conversion to the new system.

The president of a large bank in the Southwest which

172

has recently converted to automation made this statement with reference to the cost of automation changeover:

"It should be noted at this point that converting to automation does not mean an immediate reduction in expenses. On the contrary, a sharp increase occurs during the initial stages not only because of the cost of equipment, but because it is necessary to increase rather than reduce personnel.

"In this respect banks face somewhat the same predicament as the airlines when they convert from piston planes to jets. While preparing for the changeover to machine bookkeeping it is necessary for us to operate both the old and the new systems side by side until an orderly conversion can be engineered. In due course substantial savings will result, but the changeover process is an expensive one."

It should be possible to operate a bank automation system with fewer people, but the phasing out of the old system will probably be gradual and most banks will have to depend upon attrition and the normal turnover rate to reduce the total work force.

An electronic data processing system should eventually result in a substantially smaller number of employees in the operations departments of a bank, but it will probably also require a few highly skilled specialists as supervisors, programmers and operators, and these people will probably require salaries that are somewhat higher than bank salary rates under conventional bank accounting systems.

Perhaps the greatest advantage to be expected in a bank automation system is the capacity of such a system to handle a greatly increased volume of items with very little increase in cost. This desired result is a much more realistic objective than the expectation that substantial savings in direct costs will be effected.

In conclusion, it appears without doubt that bank automation in varying degrees is operating satisfactorily and efficiently in many banks, both large and small. Successful bank automation is an accomplished fact. It is no longer an experiment and is here to stay.

With most banks the question with respect to automation will be not "if" but "when," and to what degree.

CHAPTER XIII

General Operations

THE IMPORTANCE OF COMMUNICA-
TIONS to and from management and employees has been
mentioned and discussed in Chapter III in connection with
personnel administration. Equally important is the bank's
communications in various forms with its customers and
the general public. The principal media of bank communications outside the bank are mail, telephone, telegraph,
teletype, the "bank wire" and runners or messengers.

The prompt and orderly handling of both the incoming
and outgoing bank mail is an extremely important function.
It deserves careful planning and constant supervision. Frequent collection from the post office, and prompt and
careful sorting by responsible and experienced personnel
are a fundamental necessity. Where air mail "pouch service" is available, it will greatly expedite incoming air mail.

Incoming mail addressed to specific individuals or departments is of course immediately distributed to the add-
ressee, but a considerable portion of the mail will be simply
addressed to the institution, with no indication of the nature of the contents. The use of distinctively marked en-

velopes for the transit department, mail deposits and other such routine transactions will greatly speed and expedite the sort. The identification and distribution of the miscellaneous incoming mail directed to no particular individual or department requires handling by an experienced person who has a good overall knowledge of the bank's operations, and its affairs. An undue delay in getting incoming mail to the right person for handling can be both embarrassing and costly, not to mention the cause of customer dissatisfaction.

Of course incoming mail must not only be distributed promptly, but upon reaching the proper party, must be acknowledged and handled. Some banks have a standing rule that all incoming mail requiring or deserving acknowledgment, must be acknowledged on the date of receipt. If an appropriate answer cannot be given on the date of receipt, an acknowledgment is sent on that date stating that a further communication will follow as soon as possible. In the event of the absence of an officer, his mail should be promptly acknowledged by a substitute or the officer's secretary. There can be no satisfactory excuse for failure to promptly acknowledge business letters.

Banks normally require that all outgoing letters be signed by an officer, in order that someone of official standing and responsibility will make certain that the letter is well expressed and in keeping with the bank's policy. In some institutions, all letters are signed by department heads, even though they may be composed by subordinates. This is a dubious practice when it results in department heads' signing letters where they have no personal knowledge of the facts involved. It is believed to be a better practice to have such letters signed by a junior officer, who has personal knowledge of the subject, rather than have the letter prepared by a "ghost writer" and signed by a senior officer. An alternative is to have the subordinate prepare a memorandum suitable for forwarding, and upon approval of the memorandum by the senior, send it with a letter of transmittal signed by the senior, but stating the source of the memorandum and the author.

It should not be necessary to dwell on the desirability of all of a bank's letters being neat, perfect in grammar, well expressed, and a credit to the institution. It is improbable that a well managed bank will permit a careless or indifferent standard of letter writing. The practice of having an extra carbon of all letters prepared for circulation in the department not only has the virtue of keeping everyone informed as to current transactions, but also affords the department head an opportunity to observe the standards of business correspondence and take corrective action when desirable.

In recent years, a number of mechanical devices have been made available which can speed up the handling of mail. Among these are mechanical letter openers, folding machines, mailing machines which seal envelopes and imprint postage. Medium sized banks with a considerable volume of mail should keep informed concerning equipment available in this field, and use all devices that seem adaptable to the local situation.

Postage in a bank can be a considerable item of expense and is deserving of careful handling. It requires a knowledge of postal regulations and rates and a proper sense of responsibility and care. It is important to place sufficient postage on each item and equally important not to wastefully use more postage than necessary. That's a rather naive statement, but an example of what can happen is the case of a new bank mail clerk who processed several

177

thousand letters through a mailing machine without noticing that the postage meter was set at $5.00 instead of $.05 per letter.

A mailing machine can minimize the use of postage stamps and give more effective audit control of postage expense.

The time saving possibilities of the use of air mail should be understood and utilized to the full extent justified. Many banks use air mail as a matter of routine on all letters where ordinary mail will not result in delivery the following day.

The prompt distribution and dispatch of telegrams is equally as important as the proper handling of mail. The mail department or communications center is the logical central point to receive and dispatch telegrams, but telegrams which require decoding or coding must be handled by designated, responsible persons entrusted with the code.

The "bank wire" which is a telegraph system with direct connection between the larger banks in the principal cities in the country is used extensively in bank communications between the banks connected with it. For banks not connected with the bank wire, a teletype is a convenient and economical means of instantaneous communication with other banks, security dealers, and other institutions which have teletype equipment.

In the modern business world, the telephone is an indispensable tool of communication. It is used not only for conversations in the city, and at distant points, but in inter-department messages within the bank itself.

The proper use of the telephone should be a part of the training of every bank employee, including the senior executives as well as every other member of the staff. Good manners and courtesy in using the telephone are an important item in the public relations of a bank. The Bell Telephone system has prepared a manual on the proper use of the telephone which can be effectively used in any bank. A moving picture film with sound is also available for showing employees the right and wrong way to use a telephone.

The matter of proper telephone usage is a subject that must frequently be mentioned to the members of a bank staff if satisfactory performance in this respect is to be maintained. Unfortunately, a single showing of such a film or the issuance of a bulletin or oral directive will be effective but a limited time. It is a story that must be told and retold often.

The term "security" as applied to a bank, refers to all methods, procedures, and equipment for protection against robbery or burglary. It does not include protective measures against fraud or embezzlement. Every bank owes its staff the duty to provide such alarms and protective equipment as seem needed under the local conditions.

Burglar proof vaults, delayed time locks, and dual combinations are standard protective devices which are found in practically all banks. Silent, hold-up alarms which can be set off by all tellers and others in strategic locations are worth while, particularly if the alarm is given directly to a police station.

Equally as important as appropriate protective equipment is a security plan for the bank and all branches, which plan should be established after a careful study of the hazards of ambush, robbery and burglary. In every bank some one officer should be designated to assume responsibility for studying and planning the bank's security, establishing a security plan, instructing the bank staff on the security plan, and seeing that a constant state of vigilance and caution is maintained.

One of the hazards to be protected against is the possibility of early morning ambush of the first employees to arrive at the bank. There are a number of ways in which this possibility may be avoided or defeated, and the important thing is to anticipate possible situations and plan how they should be handled.

Most medium sized and large banks include uniformed guards on their staffs. The guards should be under the general supervision of the officer charged with responsibility for the bank's security, and he should see that they are thoroughly trained and properly equipped. The presence of a uniformed, armed guard in a bank is a strong deterrent to holdups and a bank guard may reasonably expect to serve indefinitely in this occupation with but little possibility of seeing an attempted robbery. A properly trained bank guard can also be very helpful to bank customers, and his alert and courteous attention can be a valuable public relations aid.

In the very small bank all supplies and equipment will ordinarily be purchased by the chief executive officer, and in a somewhat larger bank, probably by the cashier or other officer in charge of banking operations. When a bank is large enough to include a number of separate departments, it becomes desirable to centralize the purchasing function in some one other than one of the principal operating officers.

The purchasing function is frequently combined with the receipt, storage and issue of supplies. While the duties and responsibilities of purchasing agents differ widely in various banks, in some banks the position is largely concerned with records and custody of purchases, rather than in selection. The selection or choice of equipment and supplies is customarily the responsibility of department heads with the approval of the expenditures resting with an executive officer or the budget control officer.

A bank purchasing officer, by keeping well informed on sources of supply, standards of quality, price ranges and related matters, can render a valuable and needed function to a bank. By being prudent and thrifty and exercising careful and studious control over equipment and supplies, he can avoid much waste and useless expense.

CENTRAL FILES

All banks except the very smallest should maintain some type of central file in which will be indexed and cross indexed the names of all present and former customers of all kinds. Such indexed records, to have any real value, must be dependably accurate and up-to-date. The record should show at a glance the various types of business, such as checking account, savings account, loans, trust accounts, investment service, or any other type of business handled.

Sometimes the central file is maintained as a part of the credit department, or it may be an entirely separate department.

There are numerous types of mechanical equipment which can be effectively used in the preparation and maintenance of central file records. Several manufacturers produce equipment which can be used to code and key accounts so as to permit an almost endless variety of classification and mechanical sorts.

The principal objective to be obtained in a central file system is to insure an immediate and accurate answer as to whether a particular party does business with the bank, and if so, through which departments.

BANK INSURANCE

There is no acceptable yardstick by which anyone can,

with certainty, accurately measure the proper amount and kinds of insurance needed by a particular bank.

There are a number of aids and guides, however, which will be helpful in tailoring an insurance program for a bank.

The American Banking Association Bank Insurance Digest, and the check lists published by the Insurance and Surety companies are aids that should be utilized.

It is fundamental that insurance should not be considered as a substitute for adequate physical protection and controls for the reason that if losses are not minimized by proper safeguards, the costs of insurance will be increased through loss experience to prohibitive levels.

There are more than fifty different types of insurance that banks may need to protect various risks. These different types of coverage may be classified in three groups as:

1. Essential.
2. Desirable.
3. Optional.

Among the risks that are usually considered as essential for a bank are:

Fire. (with extended coverage, including windstorm and many other physical damage risks.)

Fidelity.

Liability.

Burglary and Robbery.

Forgery.

Mail.

Safe Deposit Liability.

In deciding what is essential insurance and what is merely desirable, a good rule is that any insurance for any risk which could seriously impair the soundness of a bank or seriously impede its operation is essential insurance, while insurance for risks involving potential losses that are within the bank's ability to absorb without difficulty, may be considered as desirable but not essential.

An example of insurance which is desirable but not essential is Workmen's Compensation Liability. A good example of a type of risk that may be protected by insurance, or which the bank may, at its option, elect to assume is Plate Glass Breakage.

It is desirable in every bank to have some responsible officer designated to assume responsibility for the bank insurance program and its relations with the insurers. In the small bank it may be the chief executive, but in the medium sized or larger banks it will more likely be the cashier, comptroller, or auditor. In any event, the officer so designated should be thoroughly informed on all phases of hazard insurance and constantly bear in mind the bank's particular needs in this respect.

The amount and the extent of the fidelity coverage is a matter usually determined by a resolution of the bank's Board of Directors at the annual meeting, but it is obvious that a Board will necessarily depend largely upon the recommendations of the executive officers in this respect.

The general principles of insurance coverage applicable to business firms in general, also apply to banks, but due to the nature of the banking business, there are certain types of risk which are of greater importance to banking than in other businesses.

For instance, the following classes of risk are very important in banking:

Fidelity.
Burglary and Theft.
Forgery and alteration.
Mysterious disappearance.

Misplacement.

Destruction of money, securities or documents.

Errors and omissions.

Safe Deposit liability.

Loss of mail or express.

The following types of risk are usually insured by banks, but they are risks that normally have no factors that are peculiar to banking:

Fire, and extended coverage (windstorm, explosion, etc.)

Vandalism.

Automobile. (liability, fire, theft, collision)

Elevators.

Workmen's compensation.

Plate glass.

Rental income.

Use and occupancy.

Boiler.

The need of fire insurance is so common to all individuals as well as all types of business that it does not seem necessary to stress adequate fire insurance coverage to bankers. The general principles that apply to fire coverage in other businesses, such as extended coverage, coinsurance, etc., apply with equal effect to banks.

Perhaps the single most important type of insurance to banks is the Bankers Blanket Bond. As the name implies, this type of insurance covers many types of risk, many of them but not all having to do with malfeasance or wrongdoing. The American Bankers Association, through its Insurance and Protective Committee, over a period of years, has done a great deal to broaden and clarify the protection afforded under bankers blanket bonds.

One of the many advantages of a blanket bond is that

184

it places coverage of a number of different types of risk in one insurer. Sometimes when liability insurance of different kinds is divided among more than one insurer, it is difficult to allocate a loss to one of the companies, each such company admitting the loss, but contending that it should be borne by one of the other insurers.

The Bankers Blanket Bond has amazingly broad coverage. Some of the risks which it may cover are:

1. Fidelity of employees.
2. Disappearances, destruction, or damage from practically any cause, to almost all bank personal property except furniture and equipment.
3. Forgery on checks, drafts, securities, or documents.
4. Fraud on the premises.
5. Items in transit.
6. Counterfeit currency.
7. Burglary and robbery.

In addition to the risks specifically mentioned above, there are a number of others usually covered in most blanket bonds, and quite a few more that can be included by riders which are optional.

Coverage under blanket bonds may be classified as "Primary" or "Secondary." The primary bond is basic coverage, and the secondary is excess coverage for specific hazards or a group of hazards, but is not all inclusive to the same extent as the primary coverage in that it is limited to certain types of risk. For instance, if a commercial bank has a trust department with the custody of a substantial amount of securities in fiduciary capacities, it is desirable to have a secondary bond with additional coverage for the trust assets over and above the primary bond.

There are a number of other types of insurance that are especially desirable in connection with the operation of a trust department that may not be necessary for a commercial bank that does not do a fiduciary business. An example of this sort is "errors and omissions" coverage to insure property which through error was not insured or is inadequately insured.

First class mail insurance has particular applicability to banks due to the volume of securities and other valuable papers handled by mail. Such insurance is usually cheaper than protection by registered mail.

Insurance covering any loss suffered through failure to record chattel mortgages is another type of insurance that is especially applicable to banks as well as other types of lending agencies.

Credit insurance, while widely used by many types of businesses, is not ordinarily used by banks whose primary business is concerned with the selection of credit risks.

Insurance on the life of borrowers is widely used by banks, particularly in connection with personal loans where the repayment of the loan to a considerable extent, is dependent upon the continued life of the borrower.

There are a number of limitations to the extent to which a bank may engage in the sale of insurance, and banks, in placing insurance, must be careful to handle it in the manner permitted by banking regulations.

In the lending activities of a bank there are frequently risks which should be covered by insurance other than the life of the borrower, or fire and windstorm insurance on mortgaged property. Other examples are collision and theft insurance on cars securing loans, completion or performance bonds in connection with construction loans, hazard insurance on commodities pledged as collateral and stored in warehouses, and many similar cases.

The maintenance of appropriate insurance in proper amounts is a very important function in the operation of a bank. It requires a knowledge by someone in the bank of the factors involved and a periodical check to see that coverage of all kinds is adequate. The American Institute of Banking textbook on Bank Administration has a very excellent chapter on insurance coverage for banks, and it is commended to any banker who has any duties or responsibilities in connection with insurance coverage for a bank.

CHAPTER XIV

The Audit Program

ABSOLUTE ACCURACY and conformity to banking laws and regulations are a "must" in the operation of any bank. To obtain such accuracy and conformity, two general types of supervision and control are maintained:

1. External controls by supervisory authorities such as National Bank Examiners, State Bank Examiners, Federal Reserve Examiners, Federal Deposit Insurance Corporation Examiners, and Clearing House Examiners; and

2. Internal controls such as Directors' Examining Committees, or examination by Public Accountants at the direction of a Director's Committee, and internal audit by the bank's own staff.

Much progress has been made in recent years to promote the relations and understanding between banks and the various external supervisory authorities. Bankers should understand and appreciate the important role which the supervisory authorities fulfill in our dual banking system, not only in maintaining high standards of banking operations, but in promoting the confidence of the public in banks in general.

Some bankers in the past have regarded bank examiners as a necessary nuisance that have to be endured periodically, and such an attitude was sometimes poorly concealed. A more enlightened view of bank management is that the examiners and supervisory authorities perform a useful purpose which should be reassuring and helpful to bank management. A cooperative spirit toward the examiners by bankers cannot adversely affect the bank and in some instances may result in helpful service to the bank that might not otherwise be available.

The supervisory agencies, through their national association and through conferences of various kinds with bankers have achieved a high standard of examination performance and a practical understanding of banking problems. To a large extent conflicts in jurisdiction among the various supervisory authorities have been satisfactorily adjusted.

There is a distinct difference between a bank examination by supervisory authorities and a bank audit. Both the national and state examiners fully realize the limitations on the type of examination which they are able to conduct and the examiners frequently are the cause of more effective internal audits being maintained in addition to the external examinations.

Some banks periodically have an independent audit by public accountants in addition to the regular examinations and internal audits. Such an audit in many cases will disclose situations and facts not learned through examinations and internal audits.

The principal scope of external examinations usually involves four areas of inquiry:

1. Verification of assets and liabilities.
2. Appraisal of assets.
3. Determination of conformance to banking laws and regulations.
4. Appraisal of management.

The function of the bank auditor may be expected to include:

1. The maintenance of an adequate system of accounting controls which separates operating and records functions, so that no one person handles both ends of a transaction.
2. A system of checks and balances by which various individuals and departments are balanced.
3. Verification of assets and liabilities.
4. Ascertaining that all income due is collected and properly accounted for.
5. Making certain that all expense items are proper and duly authorized.
6. Spot audits of various units from time to time.
7. Continuous audit of selected groups of transactions which will result in a daily check of such items and proof of these transactions to the general accounting records.

Another practice that is becoming increasingly used by bank auditors is direct verification of certain classes of assets and liabilities, such as deposit accounts, loans. collateral, safe-keeping accounts. This is usually accomplished by samples taken at random rather than all such accounts, unless there is some reason to suspect discrepancies. Reconcilements of balances due to and from other banks should also be obtained by the bank auditor periodically.

Since the work of the bank auditor is somewhat different in its nature from other bank officers', it calls for certain definite knowledge, experience, and personal qualifications. Since the auditor is usually responsible for reviewing, analyzing, and appraising the bank's methods, procedures, systems and policies, he necessarily must be thoroughly familiar with all phases of bank operations, not only in his own bank, but in the banking business generally. It is essential that he should be familiar with the laws and regulations governing banks, and he should know in intimate detail how the procedures in every department are handled. A bank manual of procedure is very helpful in this respect and, as suggested in Chapter II, in banks which maintain an operating manual its enforcement and keeping it current are usually functions of the bank auditor. An efficient bank auditor must be a versatile person. While he must necessarily be thoroughly versed in banking operations he must remain objective and refrain from engaging in activities which he will be called upon to check and evaluate. His close contact and association with all departments necessitates that he be a person of tact and skillful in his human relations. The fact that the auditor's duties frequently require him to correct or criticize makes it important for him to maintain a constructive attitude and not become a chronic fault finder.

The auditor must be articulate and able to express himself both orally and in writing, in a clear and concise manner since his reports sometimes may assume major importance and become public documents.

The relationship of the auditor to the Board of Directors, the chief executive, and the bank comptroller will undoubtedly vary in different banks. Generally speaking, the bank auditor should have direct access to the Board of Directors without having to go through officers whose work or records the auditor may have occasion to question or criticize. Routine reports should normally be rendered to the chief executive, but the auditor should have the unquestioned right to go directly to the Board if the situation seems to justify it.

The duty of planning systems and procedures in banks is frequently vested in an officer with the title of Comptroller instead of Auditor, and where a bank has both a comptroller and an auditor, it is very necessary that they closely coordinate their work with each other. There is no uniformity among banks as to the difference in the duties of a bank comptroller and a bank auditor, and the duties and responsibilities of each vary widely from bank to bank.

Where the comptroller is purely a planning officer and has no operating responsibilities, the auditor may report directly to the comptroller, but this should not be the case if the comptroller is responsible for functions which the auditor checks and appraises in the course of his duties.

While an auditor or his staff may be the means through which defalcations or embezzlements are uncovered, the auditing staff are not to be considered as detectives or snoopers, since this is not their primary interest, and happily for all concerned, such incidents and occurrences are infrequent.

A good auditing department can be a valuable adjunct, and a source of much comfort and help to bank management.

CHAPTER XV

The Bank Budget

BANKS DO NOT APPEAR to have adopted budgetary procedure in the management of their income and expenses to the same extent as other businesses and industries. This is somewhat surprising as banks might naturally be expected to be well organized in fiscal control matters. It is particularly surprising that some of the larger metropolitan banks do not have complete budget systems. Nevertheless, many banks, both small and large, do have some form of budgetary control and many of them have found budgets a valuable tool of management.

A proper income and expense budget for a bank must necessarily be founded upon a satisfactory and efficient general accounting system and must be coordinated with the general books in such a manner that the income and expense items of the budget are comparable with the income and expense items of the general books.

Perhaps the best method of presenting a budgetary plan for a medium sized bank will be to describe the budget system of a bank with approximately three million dollars of annual gross income, that has had a satisfactory income and expense budget for a number of years.

The bank under consideration has four separate major departments and three branch offices, but for budgetary purposes, the departments were subdivided into twenty-one sections or sub-departments including the bank's three branches. This division, of course, coincided with the departmental divisions of the general books. The bank maintains complete, detailed income and expense records for each of the twenty-one sections including overhead and indirect expense allocations to each of the divisions.

When the budget was first inaugurated, the plan was explained by the President to the officers at a meeting especially called for that purpose. The Assistant Comptroller of the bank was designated as the budget officer to supervise and coordinate the assembly of the budget data. An officer was designated as responsible for the initial data for each of the twenty-one budget divisions. In some cases, one officer, by reason of his regular duties and responsibilities, was given responsibility for more than one of the divisions of the budget.

For the information and guidance of the division officers, each was furnished with the detailed income and expense items for that division for the preceding calendar year, and since the budget preparation began on October 1st, detailed figures were also provided for the nine months elapsed in that year.

Blank forms were provided for the desired budget data, and the requested budget items corresponded with the actual reports furnished for the preceding calendar year and the current nine months' report.

A conference with each of the division officers was scheduled for a designated time with the Assistant Comptroller, in order that he might show what data he had available that would aid in the preparation of the division budgets.

Each division officer was informed that any proposed increases in the number of employees, or amount of space required, or proposed purchases of major equipment, must be accompanied by a narrative statement showing why such proposed changes in personnel, space, or equipment were believed to be necessary or desirable.

A schedule of dates for the delivery of the budget data to the Budget Officer by the division officers was also set up with the delivery dates being staggered both for the convenience of the Budget Officer, and also to allow as much time as possible for the divisions where the preparation of the budget data was believed most difficult.

Since it was realized that in many of the divisions neither the income nor the expenses followed a regular monthly average, but might be expected to vary with the seasonal cycles, each division was directed to prepare both the income and expense items by quarterly periods with the twelve month estimates to be reached by adding the items for each of the four quarterly periods. In effect, therefore, each division prepared four quarterly budgets and summed up the four to obtain the division annual budget.

The quarterly budgets were prepared for the purpose of enabling the executive officers of the bank as well as the department heads and division officers to follow the actual operating results in the ensuing year and compare the operating figures with the corresponding budget estimates each quarter.

In addition to the expenses that are allocable to certain divisions and departments, there will be certain other expenses of a general nature, such as official supervision, including directors' compensation and executives' salaries, taxes, building expense and others that should be estimated and put in the budget under the headings: general overhead, banking overhead, non-operating expenses, etc. All items of this general nature should be computed in the general accounting office by the budget officer and placed in the budget along with the division estimates.

It should be possible to estimate expenses in a bank for a given period with greater accuracy than income, for the reason that expenses can be controlled to a greater degree than income. It is to be noted that some of the divisions have service and operating functions only which do not directly produce cash income, and such divisions will, therefore, prepare an expense budget only.

The volume of deposits, the volume of loans, and trends in interest rates on both loans and investments, all of which control income, are matters that cannot be accurately forecast, even for a twelve month period. At best, such estimates will only be a guess, but with due study and thought it can be an intelligent guess.

On the other hand, bank expenses are, to a large degree, controllable, and once an expense budget is adopted, only changed circumstances or unforeseen expansion or sharp increases in price levels or wage structure should cause expenses to exceed the figures determined upon.

On the matter of salaries, the executive officers of the bank should indicate to the division heads at the time that the budget is being prepared, whether existing salary scales should be used, or whether due allowance should be made for increasing the salary level. If the management wishes to leave room in the budget for salary increases without indicating this possibility to the division heads, such an adjustment can be made by the budget officer or the executive officer after the division estimates have been assembled.

In many cases it will be desirable for the division officers to hold another conference with the budget officer when the budget estimates are delivered. Such a conference can dispose of questionable items and possible misunderstandings.

For the purposes of such a budget inter-departmental charges and credits should not be included, although they may appear on the general books and may be used and referred to in departmental reports. The reason for excluding such inter-departmental credits and charges in the general budget is that such items are normally not controllable by the department or division heads and while they may change the figures in the several departments, such items do not affect the over all income and expense situation in the bank.

The budget officer should assemble the division budget estimates and supply the overhead and general expense estimates as computed by the Comptroller and present a tentative budget to the Chief Executive of the bank.

The preliminary budget will include all suggested increases in expenses by the division heads, together with their narrative reports, explaining and justifying such increases. If the reasons or justification of increases are questionable, a conference should be held between the Chief Executive and the officer recommending such increase.

The final decision for the estimates in the budget should be made by the bank's Chief Executive. In some cases, particularly where the recommended budget includes substantial increased expenses, the Chief Executive may wish to get the approval of the Board of Directors as to the proposed increases.

At the end of each of the first three quarters, copies of

the actual income and expense figures for each of the budgetary divisions are tabulated by the Budget Officer in parallel columns with the budget estimates for the period and copies of the tabulated report are given to the executive officers, department heads, and division officers. Expense items which are materially out of line should be discussed by the Chief Executive with the department head responsible for such expense.

Since the budget is prepared by quarters, if developments occur after the beginning of the fiscal year which make it apparent that the budget estimates for either income or expense should be adjusted either upward or downward, this can be accomplished without any difficulty, and the revised estimates can be incorporated into a revised budget. The budget report for the first three quarters of a fiscal year will prove very useful in preparing the estimates for the next fiscal year which will normally be prepared in the last quarter of the current year.

While there should be nothing sacred in budget estimates and there is every reason to suppose that there will be justifiable variations on both the income and expense side when comparing the estimates with the actual operating results, nevertheless, there are a number of advantages which can and should result from such budgets.

On the income side the estimates can provide a goal or quota for department heads to seek. On the expense side it tends to make department heads and division heads expense conscious, and provides a yard stick with which to measure results.

A specimen of a budget report for a full fiscal year is shown in Chart "A". The report for each of the three quarters of the year would be similar in form with the reports for the second and third quarters being cumulative in that they also include the figures for the preceding quarters in the fiscal year. A completed budget estimate for a specific department as presented to the Budget Officer, is shown in Chart "B" on page 202.

Experience with this type of budgetary procedure has proven that it involves no direct expense and from management's viewpoint, it more than justifies the time and effort required by the staff in the program.

CHART "B"

TENTATIVE BUDGET
TRUST DEPARTMENT

INCOME	FIRST QUARTER	SECOND QUARTER	THIRD QUARTER	FOURTH QUARTER	TOTALS
Trust Fees	$30,000.00	$29,000.00	$34,000.00	$82,000.00	$175,000.00
EXPENSES					
Salaries	25,000.00	25,000.00	25,000.00	25,000.00	100,000.00
Stationery and Printing	900.00	1,000.00	900.00	900.00	3,700.00
Postage, Express and Insurance	300.00	275.00	275.00	300.00	1,150.00
Legal Expense	375.00	375.00	375.00	375.00	1,500.00
Equipment, Repairs and Upkeep	300.00	300.00	300.00	300.00	1,200.00
Furniture and Fixtures	300.00	200.00	300.00	200.00	1,000.00
Fidelity and Other Bonds	250.00	250.00	250.00	250.00	1,000.00
Telephone and Telegraph	700.00	630.00	600.00	700.00	2,630.00
Subscriptions and Memberships	200.00	375.00	225.00	200.00	1,000.00
Traveling	400.00	100.00	100.00	200.00	800.00
Advertising	750.00	650.00	600.00	600.00	2,600.00
Social Security Taxes	763.00	560.00	425.00	350.00	2,098.00
Automobile Expenses	175.00	225.00	150.00	150.00	700.00
Miscellaneous Expense	100.00	100.00	100.00	100.00	400.00
Examinations				1,500.00	1,500.00
Total Expenses	$30,513.00	$30,040.00	$29,600.00	$31,125.00	$121,278.00
Estimated Net Income					$53,722.00

CHAPTER XVI

Trust Department

TRUST BUSINESS has been aptly defined as "the management of property of others." Property, of course, is used in the broad sense and more often than not is personal property in the form of securities rather than real property.

It is a well accepted fact among bankers that trust business in the United States has not been a very profitable business for most banks. The commercial bank with a trust department that consistently operates at a profit is an exception rather than the rule, and is principally limited to banks that have built up a sizable volume of trust assets and whose trust fees are realistic.

The large metropolitan banks which have a good volume of corporate trust business probably enjoy a better ratio of trust profits than any other group of banks, but the possibilities of a volume of corporate trust business in most medium sized banks are definitely limited.

As a matter of fact, the majority of medium sized banks which operate trust departments do not have accurate departmental cost accounting and therefore do not accurately know whether they are making a profit, and if so, how much. A system of simplified trust department cost accounting has been prepared by the Committee on Costs and Charges of the Trust Division of the American Bankers Association, and it is recommended to any bank that does not have a satisfactory system of computing its trust income and expense.

There are far more banks in America that have trust powers and are legally authorized to engage in a trust business than are actively exercising those powers. There are also many banks that are nominally in the trust business with a part time trust staff but whose trust business is very insignificant.

The operation of a trust department by a bank cannot successfully be a half hearted matter. The job should be well done or left alone.

One of the difficulties in maintaining and operating a successful trust department is the matter of a fully qualified staff. Trust operations require specialists and technicians in a number of different fields such as law, accounting, taxes, investments, real estate, business management, etc. Such qualifications are seldom found in one or two persons, and a staff of several specialists is therefore required if the various requirements are to be adequately met. Such a well qualified staff is just as much needed for a few accounts as many, yet the average bank, just beginning a trust business, can ill afford a complete trust staff with only a small income from that source.

It is not very difficult to outline on paper the desirable qualities of a trust officer, but having determined the desired ideal, the location of such a paragon of excellence in the flesh, and who is available, is apt to be a fruitless search.

Perhaps the most desirable quality in a trust officer is

the *ability to inspire confidence*. This is an intangible characteristic that results from many separate factors, but it is highly important since no matter how competent a trust officer might be, unless he can inspire a feeling of confidence in customers and associates, his work will lack effectiveness. Of course, the ability to inspire confidence must be backed up with ability to perform since unjustified confidence will only lead to difficulties.

Twenty-five years ago it was the fashion for banks to employ lawyers as trust officers, and most of the senior trust officers of that time had formerly practiced law. Since that time, the definition of "the practice of law" has been broadened to include many transactions, such as drafting wills that trust officers formerly performed as a matter of course. Court decisions and joint agreements between Bar Associations and Bankers Associations have resulted in a general agreement with reference to the activities of lawyers employed by corporate fiduciaries. The agreed upon principles greatly restrict the legal work that may be performed by lawyers in the employ of corporations.

This may be one of the reasons why a smaller proportion of trust officers are lawyers than was true a generation ago; in any event, there seems to be a trend away from the employment of lawyers in the trust business and the use of outside legal counsel whenever legal service is needed.

The maintenance of good relations with the local bar is of great importance to any bank conducting a trust business, since lawyers can be very influential with their clients in choosing a fiduciary. If lawyers are included in a trust department staff, it is highly important that they fully understand the limitations concerning the practice of law by corporate fiduciaries.

Since trust business is primarily concerned with the

management of investments, it would seem that while a knowledge of law is helpful, investment experience and skill is the primary qualification needed.

While the knowledge qualifications in the fields of investments, law, taxes, accounting, real estate, and business management are important, there are certain personal qualifications that are also important. The desirability of inspiring confidence has already been stressed. Close behind this quality should come an interest in people. A trust officer who does not have an abiding interest in people and a desire to serve them will probably not be a successful trust administrative officer, regardless of how great his technical knowledge qualifications.

One of the suspicions and criticisms leveled at corporate fiduciaries is that they are heartless corporations, lacking in the milk of human kindness. Those who know the record of corporate trusteeship in America, know that this accusation of lack of personal interest is not true. The story of the administration of personal trusts in this country is a heart warming one, full of countless hundreds of instances where trust officers have displayed personal devotion and interest far above the call of duty.

If personal trust business is to continue this fine record the personal equation in the performance of the trust officer's duties must continuously be stressed. A dispassionate performance of routine duties, regardless of how technically perfect, will not suffice. Patience, tolerance, and human understanding of the viewpoint of others are a necessary part of the attitude of a trust officer in dealing with his customers.

Mention has already been made of the importance of relations between banks doing a trust business and members of the bar. Life insurance underwriters are another group whom trust officers should know and cultivate since they also can be very helpful in trust new business development.

In many of the larger cities joint councils have been organized by life underwriters and trust men for a cooperative program and the discussion of matters of mutual interest. In some cities such councils have been broadened to include lawyers and accountants, as well as life underwriters and trust men. All of these groups are important to trust men and cordial relations should be fostered and maintained.

One of the most important developments in trust business during the present generation is a procedure known as "estate planning". It involves the study and analysis of a person's property with the view of arranging the most beneficial and economical use of the property by all members of the owner's family.

Such planning involves a number of specific skills, all of which are seldom found in one individual. For this reason estate planning is usually best performed by a team of specialists, each of whom contributes different talents and knowledge. The "estate planning team" is normally composed of:

1. The owner of the property who has detailed knowledge of its extent and the purposes which he wishes to accomplish.

2. The property owner's lawyer who should be the key figure on the team since it is his responsibility to put the plan into proper legal language and to be responsible for its legal effect and tax consequences.

3. A life insurance counselor, since life insurance is apt to be an important part of any estate plan.

4. An accountant who is familiar with, or will have ac-

cess to the property owner's financial records, including the nature and extent of all of his holdings, his previous tax returns, and the valuation basis of his assets.

5. A trust officer who is experienced in financial and investment management and trust and estate administration.

While the lawyer member of the team might rightfully be considered as the "Captain" since there are certain responsibilities to his client that he cannot delegate or avoid, the trust officer might well be considered the coordinator since he must have considerable knowledge of the work of the other three specialists and must frequently serve the function of expediting the planning to a conclusion.

The trust officer member, perhaps more than any other member of the estate planning "team", should have an acute awareness of the respective fields of the members of the group and the importance of each specialist respecting the prerogatives of the others.

Estate planning should be considerably more than merely seeking ways and means of minimizing taxes, although this feature is usually important. In addition to a full knowledge of the possibilities to be achieved through intelligent estate planning, the trust officer should also be aware of its limitations and not be guilty of overselling either his own capabilities or those of the institution he represents. The two most authoritative sources of information on estate planning are "An Estate Planner's Handbook" by the late Mayo Adams Shattuck and James F. Farr, and "Estate Planning" by James Casner, both books being published by Little Brown & Company of Boston.

The decision to venture into the trust business is not one to be made lightly and without a full appreciation of the obligations it incurs. There is perhaps no other type of business where the compensation bears such a low ratio to the potential liability, and where the minimum operating expenses require such a high volume of business.

It is somewhat difficult to accurately discuss and measure volume of trust business because the yardsticks used are not uniform. The method most frequently employed is book value of trust assets, but this is full of loopholes. For instance, book value may represent market value at time of initial inventory, or it may include all non par stocks at $1.00 per share, and in various banks and various accounts it has many different bases that mitigate against comparisons.

In some banks, assets handled in safekeeping or custody accounts are included in the volume of personal trust business while in others they are excluded.

Perhaps the best unit of comparison between trust departments of different banks is dollars of cash fees collected annually. Such a method can include both personal and corporate trust business.

In the past some attempts have been made to establish some "rules of thumb" about the ratio of the number of trust department employees to the volume of trust assets, but such ratios can have no significance without an accepted standard of valuing trust assets. It is also true that there is but little significance and relationship between the valuation of the assets of a trust account and the number of man hours required annually to handle it. The nature of the assets, the tax problems, other problems involved, the needs of the beneficiaries and even the personal characteristics of the customers themselves can make the widest difference in the administration of two trust accounts of equal dollar evaluation.

Some bank executives have estimated that the ratio of trust employees should be approximately one employee to each million dollars of personal trust assets, but this rule of thumb would only be applicable within certain limits at both extremes, and as mentioned above, the manner of valuing the trust assets might play an important part in the ratio.

If one fundamental principle in connection with the operation of a trust department is worthy of being stressed more than any other, it is the policy of avoiding any form, fashion or semblance of self-dealing. It is elementary that a fiduciary cannot serve two masters, and therefore cannot do business with itself in an individual or corporate capacity to any extent whatsoever. A bank in a fiduciary capacity should not have any financial interest, direct or indirect, in any property of any kind bought for, or sold to a trust account which it is handling, and likewise, it should not purchase for itself any property from any of its trusts.

"A Statement of Principles of Trust Institutions" adopted by the Trust Division of the American Bankers Association in 1933 contains the following expression:

"It is the duty of a trustee to administer a trust solely in the interest of the beneficiaries without permitting the intrusion of interests of the trustee or third parties that may in any way conflict with the interests of the trust."

The executive officers of a national bank or a member bank of the Federal Reserve System operating a trust department should be thoroughly familiar with the provisions of Regulation F of the Federal Reserve System relating to the operation of trust departments.

A commercial bank which does not exercise trust powers should study carefully the situation and realize fully the responsibilities it will necessarily assume if it embarks in the trust business. As suggested above, trust work should not be undertaken without an adequate, well trained staff. The potential income is low as compared with the potential liability and the theoretical benefits of holding and attracting commercial business or keeping up with a competitor in service, are not, in themselves, sufficient reasons for entering the fiduciary field. There are many banks which have glibly undertaken to provide trust service without fully realizing what they were getting into. Once trusts are accepted, it may prove to be "a bear by the tail" because it is not always possible to resign and give up the responsibility.

A recent study of Trust Department profits and expenses conducted by the Federal Reserve Bank in the Sixth District, reached the conclusion that trust departments can expect to break even at about 40 million dollars of trust assets or about 150,000 dollars of fees and commissions.

There are many strong and convincing arguments why a corporate fiduciary should be more efficient and satisfactory than an individual. Likewise, a successful career as a trust officer can be a most satisfying and rewarding experience, but both the individual and the institution, to be successful in this field, must be well equipped for the job.

CHAPTER XVII

Safe Deposit Operation

ALTHOUGH NEARLY EVERY COMMER-
CIAL BANK except the very smallest has safe deposit boxes available for customers, there is probably no department of banking to which top management devotes so little thought and attention.

Even a casual reading of some of the leading court decisions prescribing the degree of responsibility of a bank providing safe deposit service should convince a bank executive, not only of the importance of fully understanding the bank's duty and potential liability, but of the necessity of setting up sound procedures and maintaining constant close supervision of safe deposit operations.

The first responsibility of management with respect to the safe deposit department is a clear understanding of the nature of the relationship between the bank and the customers using safe deposit boxes.

The laws of the several states differ as to the status of banks conducting a safe deposit business. In some states the courts have determined the relationship to be that of Landlord and Tenant, but in most states the courts have held that the safe deposit business is governed by the law of bailment.

Since the law applicable to bailments usually imposes a higher degree of responsibility than in the case of Landlord and Tenant, it is to the bank's advantage to establish a Landlord relationship instead of a bailment, if the laws of the state in question permit it. Where the state laws are silent on the subject, or permit the bank to rent safe deposit boxes under a contract establishing a Landlord-Tenant relationship, this should be done by means of a carefully drawn contract prepared by the bank's attorney.

If under the laws of your state, a bailment relationship exists, it means that the bank is considered to be in constructive possession of the contents of every box rented. This relationship requires the highest degree of care in establishing and carrying out sound operating procedures. The best defense when confronted with a claim, is to be able to establish affirmative proof that the safe deposit department has been operated with the utmost degree of care and that the bank has not been negligent in any manner.

In lawsuits against banks based on loss or disappearance of property from safe deposit boxes, the courts in nearly all instances have been harsh in the standards of performance required by banks. Even in the absence of positive proof of negligence by the bank, courts have often referred the decision to a jury to determine whether there is any evidence from which it could reasonably be inferred that the bank failed to exercise the utmost precaution to prevent loss to the box renter. Under such circumstances, there is no effective substitute for sound management and careful operating procedures.

Some small banks, in an attempt to avoid the high

degree of care required in the usual safe deposit relationship, have allowed customers to use safe deposit boxes without charge in the belief that the absence of a charge would avoid liability. It seems well established that neither the absence of a charge or a contract limiting liability can absolve a bank if negligence is proven.

The subject of prudent, efficient safe deposit operations has been given careful attention by the members of the American Safe Deposit Association. Among bankers who have specialized in safe deposit operations, certain fundamental principles are recognized which all banks who engage in the safe deposit business should carefully consider and follow if possible. Among the recommended practices are:

1. The vault door, the vault wall construction, and the individual boxes and locks must be physically sound and kept in good mechanical order.

2. The personnel of the safe deposit department must be of the same high caliber as others holding responsible positions in the bank. The positions require skill in human relations, dependability in faithfully following established procedures, accuracy with records, and unquestioned integrity. The Safe Deposit Department is not an appropriate place for superannuated employees who cannot hold other bank jobs, or marginal employees who have been unsatisfactory in other assignments.

3. The outside vault door should have dual combination locks and be equipped with a time lock. A permanent record should be maintained with the signatures of two bank representatives who witness the opening of the vault in the morning and who witness the setting of the time lock and the closing of the vault door in the afternoon.

4. Each safe deposit box should require the use of

two keys to gain entrance. One of these keys will be the vault attendant's key (never to be referred to as a "pass key") kept by the bank's representative and the other key will be the customer's key.

5. The box rental agreement should be in writing on a form approved by the bank's attorney.

6. A permanent signature file of box renters must be maintained. To gain entrance to a box, the renter should be required to sign an entry slip each time and present the entry slip with the key to the attendant. The attendant, before permitting entry, should verify the signature on the entry slip with that on the signature card to make sure that the number of the key and the signature conform with the bank's records. This is important even if the attendant personally knows the customer, since customers sometimes innocently get in possession of the wrong key. A procedure that requires the attendant to note the date of entry in the signature file on the occasion of every entry is desirable, since it will automatically cause the attendant to check the signature and key number at each time of entry.

7. The attendant should place both keys in the box lock, open the door, remove the container in the presence of the customer return the customer's key to him and either hand the container to the customer, or carry it to a customer's booth, making certain, however, that the attendant does not have possession of the container except in the presence of the customer. The box door should be closed and locked while the container is out to prevent the possibility of a wrong container being returned to a box. When the customer is ready to return the container to the box, he should again give the key to the attendant who will

open the box door, see that the container is placed in the box and the door securely locked.

8. Since knowledge of the contents of a box may adversely affect the bank's liability in the event of a claim, it is important that neither the attendant nor any representative of the bank should have any knowledge of the contents of a customer's box. For the same reason it is imprudent for an officer or employee of the bank to act as a deputy or licensee of a box renter for the purpose of entering a safe deposit box for the customer.

9. It should be standard practice for the vault attendant to inspect booths for forgotten items or articles that might have been dropped on the floor after each use of a booth and before the customer leaves the department.

10. Perhaps the greatest hazard in connection with the operation of a safe deposit business is the possibility of unauthorized entry into a customer's box. Every possible care and safeguard must be exercised at all times to prevent any possibility of unauthorized entry. As far as it is possible to do so, the system must be such that unauthorized entry cannot occur under any circumstances.

11. Locks should be changed each time when a box is vacated before it is leased to another tenant.

12. Keys to unrented boxes should be kept under the dual control of two bank officers.

13. No officers or employees of the bank should be permitted to retain keys to a rented box for any reason whatsoever. Any keys to safe deposit boxes that might be found or delivered to bank employees should immediately be delivered to the bank Auditor to be placed under dual control. At the time of receiving such a key the Auditor should obtain an affidavit from the bank representative as to the circumstances under which he or she came into

possession of the key and affirmatively stating that the key had not been used to gain entrance into the box.

14. Vault attendants must be thoroughly instructed as to the proper procedures under special circumstances such as:

a. Entry of a deceased renter's box for the purpose of looking for a will.

b. Giving possession of a box to a deceased renter's executor or administrator upon delivery of Letters of Administration.

c. Noting the death of a box renter on the signature records and the consequent revocation of any deputies.

d. Proper authority for changes in authorized signatures by corporations and associations.

e. Procedures in case of the death of a joint tenant.

f. Procedure in case of the mental incompetency of a box renter.

g. Procedure for drilling a box when authorized and necessary.

Safe deposit box rents are normally collected in advance, but upon the expiration of the initial rental period a bill for the next period should be promptly rendered and a systematic collection procedure followed.

Both the safe deposit department procedures as well as the box rental accounting records should be frequently checked by the Auditing Department. In the event the procedures are not prudent or sound, or if the approved procedures are not being scrupulously followed, a prompt report should be made by the Auditing Department to top management.

Since the maximum rental that can be received from safe deposit boxes is small when compared to the almost unlimited potential liability, it behooves the management of a bank to use every possible caution in its safe deposit box procedures to avoid liability, and even then to protect against such liability by appropriate insurance coverage.

For a comprehensive discussion of safe deposit operation, and a good check list of safe deposit operation procedures, bank executives are referred to Chapter X of the *Manual of Bank Accounting, Auditing and Operation*, published by the National Association of Bank Auditors and Comptrollers.

CHAPTER XVIII

Public Relations

IN RECENT YEARS no phase of business activity has been more discussed and emphasized than the subject of public relations. This is true not only in the banking business, but in all lines of business and industry. Even the learned professions such as doctors and lawyers have recognized the importance of public relations in their professional practice.

Literally tons of reading matter and various forms of communication have been devoted to the subject of public relations. Almost every business convention devotes a part of the program to some phase of the subject.

Public relations has so many facets that it is a topic that can never be exhausted. It is a term that means many different things to different people. While "public relations" has been defined many, many times, it is difficult to find a short, concise definition that is descriptive and all inclusive. No one definition appears entirely adequate, since to some extent public relations is "all things to all people."

One definition that seems reasonably satisfactory is

"Public relations is an attitude and course of action designed to win public favor and acceptance."

The past generation was one of tremendous technical and mechanical improvement. Every business and industry has made tremendous advances and improvement in its equipment.

The present generation has become increasingly aware that we have not made as much improvement in our human relations as we have in our mechanical techniques. This is just as true of banking as in other lines of endeavor. Too often, we have assumed that our people engaged in routine banking assignments would acquire skill in human relations without any specific training or direction in this field, but unfortunately, this is not always true.

In the latter part of the nineteenth century, "the public be damned" was typical of the attitude of many business executives, but in the twentieth century business men generally have come to realize that favorable public opinion constitutes a valuable business asset. It is now generally recognized that human attitudes have a significant effect upon business success.

Bankers of former years seldom enjoyed good public relations. The typical banker as pictured in cartoons and the press was a florid, paunchy individual with a cutaway coat and a high silk hat. The legion of stories such as the banker with the glass eye, and the father who was unwilling to have his daughter wed a banker, are well known to every one who was engaged in banking in the early thirties.

Banking probably reached the low ebb of its popularity in 1932 when President Roosevelt made his epochal remark about driving the money changers out of the temple. It is perhaps significant that the first manual on bank public relations was published by the American Bankers Association a year after that in 1933, in cooperation with the Financial Advertisers Association.

During World War II bankers did outstanding work, not only in the promotion and sale of war bonds, but also in the financing of the war effort generally. All of these activities resulted in greatly improved public relations for banking at the close of the war period. Since then, bankers in increasing measure have realized the value of continuing to cultivate a favorable public opinion.

There are several groups of people (with some of the groups overlapping) whose attitudes as a group have a direct effect upon the public relations of a bank. These groups are:

1. Employees.
2. Depositors and other customers.
3. The public in the trade area of the bank.
4. Stockholders.
5. The general public.

Of the five groups mentioned, unquestionably the bank employees are the group which in largest measure will determine the public attitude toward a bank. Since the scope and quality of service in most banks does not usually differ to a great degree, the principal difference between banks is the way the staff treat the customers and the public.

A sound bank public relations program must necessarily be founded upon good relations between the bank management and its employees. Bank employees cannot be expected to have the right sort of attitude in dealing with the public if the employees themselves have not had the right sort of treatment from management. The composite attitude of the public will result from what the employees think, say, and do—not only in the bank, but outside the bank as well. Everything that any member of a bank staff says or does, helps the public form an opinion about the bank. The bank's effort should be devoted toward seeing that what the staff say and do will cause a favorable impression.

A public relations program in a bank has at least two primary aspects—first, giving good service, and second, informing the public concerning those services. While there are a great many elements of public relations, all of them are in one way or another concerned with one or both of the two factors mentioned above.

The need for good performance is, of course, of paramount importance. No amount of lip service, ballyhoo, advertising, or gimmicks can be a substitute for good performance and service which pleases the customers.

Just as good public relations are built upon good performance, good performance must be built upon the right attitude of the bank staff.

The beginning point in building a good employee attitude is to create staff interest through good staff communication. Employees should be fully informed about subjects important to the bank, such as policies, operations, services, and objectives. If employees are expected to be good team members, they must be treated like members of the team by giving them full information.

Bank policies are determined by management, but they must be executed and carried out by the staff. Effective execution is doubtful unless the staff clearly understands the policies and the reasons therefor, and are fully sympathetic.

The public relations program for any bank must be tailor-made to fit its specific needs and situation. The beginning of such a program should be a soul searching survey of self-analysis to determine:

1. The existing situation.
2. The proposed objectives.
3. The procedure for reaching the objectives.

The research incident to planning such a program must be done by people who are fully competent to diagnose conditions and prescribe the measures needed. In many banks this can be done by staff members who are competent in their field, and this is desirable where it is possible. If the bank does not have anyone who can do a good job in this respect, professional consultants are available who can be employed, but in any event it is a procedure that must be followed if a good program is to be intelligently planned and carried out.

A good public relations program is not something that just accidentally happens or that is an automatic by-product of providing courteous, efficient service. It inevitably must be the product of careful research and planning, and sustained follow-up.

The importance of effective communications to the employee staff has already been mentioned. Effective communications, both with the employee group and with the public should be a two-way process. The bank should not only publicize what it is doing, but it should also listen to what others are saying about its performance.

The two principal channels of communication of a bank with the community and the general public are publicity and advertising. By the term "publicity," we mean news releases in newspapers or other publications, or news releases through radio or television. Such publicity is to be distinguished from paid advertising and the two should never be confused.

All publicity material should be carefully checked for news value and readability and the bank's relations with newsmen should not be strained by attempting to disguise advertising as publicity.

Every bank should have some responsible officer who is charged with responsibility for relations with the press. If the bank representatives can learn the techniques of properly preparing news releases, this can be a valuable public relations asset to the bank.

Good advertising like any other well executed program, requires good planning. The larger banks find it desirable to employ the skill and experience of a professional advertising man on the staff or else utilize the services of an established advertising agency.

A bank that does not feel justified in employing an advertising specialist or using an agency can obtain a fairly complete bank advertising service from the Advertising Department of the American Bankers Association.

One elementary principle to be borne in mind by any person responsible for selecting the advertising media for any institution is that there are hundreds of good media of advertising and no single institution can use all of them. The determination of an advertising program, therefore, necessitates the selection of the subjects and manner of presentation that seem best adapted to the objectives sought.

Any one charged with the responsibility of handling advertising for a bank should by all means read the chapter on advertising in the American Institute of Banking textbook on Public Relations.

Selling is an important part of banking although a bank has nothing to sell but its service. At one time a proposal for personal solicitation by bank staff members would have been considered quite a revolutionary idea, but today there is a tendency throughout banking to enlist bank officers in a systematic plan of calling on customers and prospective customers. The results of such programs in most banks have been gratifying. While a customer calling program should be sponsored by the highest level in bank management, the actual calling should be decentralized to include as many of the staff as practicable.

Within recent years a great change has taken place in the type of annual statement made by banks to their stockholders. This is especially true among medium sized banks. Until after World War II, the December 31st statement of nearly all except the big city banks, was a condensed balance sheet statement with perhaps a few paragraphs of comment concerning the year's earnings and business conditions. Sometimes a multigraphed copy of the President's comments made at the annual stockholders' meeting would accompany the year-end balance sheet figures. The distribution of such statements was largely limited to the bank's shareholders and it was intended literally to be just as the name implied, a statement to stockholders.

The modern trend is to make the annual statement a great deal more than just a statement to stockholders. In many cases, it is frankly a selling piece, designed to "sell" the bank, not only to the stockholders, but to the employees, the customers, and the general public.

The old type of statement has been superseded by elaborately illustrated booklets with colored pictures, graphs, and every attention-compelling device known in modern advertising technique.

While there may be some question as to the desirability and justification of some of the more ornate and elaborate bank statements, the trend toward attractive illustrated statements is believed to be a forward step.

Bankers who are interested in revising or improving their reports to stockholders can profit from reading the Graduate School of Banking thesis of Spencer S. Marsh, Jr., entitled "A Bank's Annual Report To Its Stockholders." This thesis may be obtained by members of the American Bankers Association from its library.

In addition to its efforts in direct selling in a community a bank should promote its public relations by being a good citizen in the community. This entails the bank staff's assuming leadership in community affairs. Such leadership should be participated in by as many of the bank's staff as is possible.

A bank's policies, operations, and participation in community affairs can have a tremendous effect on the progress and growth of a community. Such participation in community affairs should include the colleges and schools at all educational levels as well as civic, charitable, and religious organizations.

Many publications have been devoted to the subject of Bank Public Relations. Two books, both published in 1956 on this prolific subject are "Public Relations For Your Bank," published by the American Institute of Banking, and "The Bank and Its Public" by Robert Lindquist of Chicago, published by Harper and Brothers. Both of these books are orthodox, well organized, and well presented. They are both recommended as desirable reading for all bankers.

CHAPTER XIX

Inter-Bank Relationships

ALTHOUGH BANKS ACTIVELY COM-
PETE with each other, they are also mutually dependent
upon each other to a greater extent than most competing
firms in other lines of business. Banks must have an agreed-
upon plan for crediting and debiting items on each other
and it is also to their mutual benefit to exchange credit
information and cooperate in other ways.

There is but little literature available on the subject
of correspondent banking as compared with the wealth of
information in circulation on most other banking subjects.
Opinions, theories, and philosophies of banks and bankers
with reference to correspondent bank relationships vary
perhaps more widely than on any other phase of banking.
It is likewise a part of banking that does not seem to have
had as careful planning as most subjects.

Obviously, correspondent banking has two principal
sides—depositing funds with other banks in anticipation of
needed services, and receiving deposits from other banks
for which they will expect some form of service. Most

banks, except the smallest, engage in both sides of such activity.

Both the receiving of bank deposits from other banks, and the deposit of funds with correspondent banks, deserve careful analysis and planning.

The principal forms of service which banks render to other banks are:

1. *COLLECTION SERVICE*

Collection of checks, drafts, notes, trade acceptances, commercial paper, bonds, coupons, and other items.

2. *INVESTMENT SERVICE*

Investment information and advice, buying and selling securities, custody of securities.

3. *FOREIGN TRANSACTIONS*

Transfers by wire or cable to all parts of the world, also information and aid on foreign transactions.

4. *CREDITS AND LOANS*

Supplying credit information and assistance on loans, including participations in loans.

5. *SUPPLYING CURRENCY OR COIN*

In addition to the above more commonly used services, banks frequently give specialized help and assistance to correspondent banks in such matters as appraisals, tax information and advice, operating equipment and procedures, training of officers and employees, trust service, and other phases of banking.

In planning a correspondent bank program, the bank should determine which of the above types of service it will need, and which banks can most reasonably be expected to efficiently render the services needed. The next point to be decided is what average balances will be required with the banks chosen to adequately compensate them for the services expected. A tentative schedule of such balances should be maintained with the expectation that changes and adjustments will be made from time to time in accordance with shifting balances of business. The matter of such appropriate average balances should be a matter of free discussion between the banks concerned with the bank rendering the service indicating its costs and the break-even point.

On the other side of the picture, a bank seeking deposits from other banks must realistically determine its trade area and what services it can profitably perform for other banks. A correspondent banking relationship should be mutually satisfactory to both banks with each receiving some benefit from the arrangement.

Correspondent bank balances received on a mere courtesy basis without any resulting benefits to the depositing bank, are not apt to be permanent or sizable. In soliciting correspondent bank deposits the soliciting bank should have something more tangible to offer than hand shaking and fellowship.

An analysis of the correspondent bank deposits throughout America would undoubtedly reveal that many banks maintain such accounts that are entirely without banking justification. Often such accounts have been opened as a result of personal friendships, or as an outcome of a particular business transaction, and there is no real continuing need for the deposit. Such deposits are an extravagant use of the bank's funds. Periodically, a bank should review its list of funds due from other banks to see if the list should not be curtailed. On the other hand, as banks grow and expand, and use the services of their correspondents to a greater degree, they should expect to increase their compensating balances proportionately. It is a relationship that should be adjusted with current conditions and not be permitted to remain static.

This subject should not be dismissed without some mention of some of the wasted efforts and extravagant practices in connection with correspondent bank practices. While calling on customers is a well established practice among aggressive banks and has much to be said in its favor, there is much ineffectual calling among correspondent banks. Perhaps the most conspicuous weakness is in the use of representatives for such calls who are ill equipped to do anything but make a purely social call. While such social calls, if not too frequent, do no harm, neither are they likely to accomplish any worth while results.

A representative calling on a correspondent bank should first of all be well equipped with a general knowledge of banking, particularly the field in which the customer bank is interested. He should have an intimate knowledge of the balances maintained, the type and volume of the services rendered and the realistic potential of other services that might be utilized to advantage. The interview should be centered around the relationship between the two banks and the service to be rendered rather than an exchange of pleasantries.

The visiting banker should be conscious of the other man's time and the possibility that he has many other callers on a similar mission. Too long a call when there is really nothing to be said or accomplished can often do more harm than good.

Attempts to cultivate correspondent bank relationships through lavish entertainment at conventions, theater tickets, elaborate Christmas gifts, and personal favors and attention are not apt to result in mutually profitable business, the only sound basis on which to build.

CHAPTER XX

Bank Capitalization

"THE FIRST FUNCTION of bank capital is to protect the depositors and any other creditors. The second function of bank capital is to earn and pay an adequate return to its owners."*

While a great deal has been written and said concerning appropriate ratios of bank capital to deposits and to risk assets, there is very little literature available on the subject of appropriate balances between the items which compose a bank's capital structure.

A bank's capital funds normally consist of four items:
1. Capital Stock.
2. Surplus.
3. Undivided Profits.
4. Reserves (other than tax reserves or other definite accrued liabilities).

In speaking of bank capital and in computing capital ratios, usually all four of the above items are included within the general term "capital."

"In deciding how much 'capital' (e.g., capital stock,

---

*New York State Bankers Association, Report of Risk Asset Ratio Committee.

surplus, undivided profits and reserves) a bank should have, an appropriate answer is that the bank's capital should equal or exceed the amount of its 'risk assets', multiplied by the degree of risk to which they are subject. This raises the questions:—What assets are subject to risk, and how much risk?" *

These questions are often difficult to answer accurately as to a given bank.

The two most common reasons for increasing the total amount of a bank's capitalization are:

1. Additional protection of the bank's depositors.
2. The increase of the legal lending limit of the bank in order to take care of its customers' credit requirements.

The accomplishment of the first objective obviously requires an addition to the capital structure from sources outside the capital items, while the second objective can be accomplished to the extent that available funds may be transferred from undivided profits or reserves to surplus or capital stock. It is clear that a transfer from surplus to capital stock does not aid in the accomplishment of either objective.

There seems to be no generally accepted formula for the division of the components of a bank's capital structure. When the "double liability" factor was applicable to bank stock, it was considered highly desirable that the surplus be at least equivalent to the capital stock for protection against possible assessment against the stockholders. When this law was repealed, a new regulation was substituted to the effect that if the surplus is less than capital, 10% of each year's earnings must be added to surplus before the declaration of dividends. A few banks carry the surplus-

* Illinois Bankers Assocaition, "The Problems of Adequate Bank Capital."

capital ratio to the extreme, and surplus is sometimes as high as ten times the capital stock. The First National Bank of New York was a notable case of this type of capitalization until it revised its capital structure shortly before its merger with National City Bank of New York. There do not appear to be any very sound reasons for having such a high ratio of surplus to capital stock.

The general practice over the country seems to be that surplus is somewhat in excess of capital stock. The composite ratio of surplus and capital stock in all commercial banks in the United States, expressed in percentages of surplus to total assets, and capital to total assets, is approximately 3% and 2% respectively.

New banks which have not had a reasonable opportunity to build up surplus out of earnings usually have a low ratio of surplus to capital, and in such cases a large percentage of earnings must be retained until surplus is equivalent to capital.

The undivided profits account in banks is usually considerably less than the capital stock or surplus. Traditionally the officers responsible for the management of a bank like to maintain a comfortable undivided profits account, and are more conservative in their willingness to distribute earnings in the form of cash dividends than either directors or stockholders. Management frequently needs funds for expansion and improvements, and undivided profits is the most convenient fund to draw on for such items, therefore, the management officers like to have a convenient backlog of undivided profits to take care of contingencies that are not provided for by reserve accounts.

Prior to World War II, the ratio of capital to deposits was considered a significant measure, and the rule of one to ten was generally accepted as a proper criterion. The tremendous increase in deposits, and the accompanying heavy increase in U. S. Government securities owned by commercial banks, has produced a general agreement that the old ratio of one to ten is no longer appropriate.

If the banks with a capital ratio below the national average increase their capital in an attempt to equal the average, each such increase will raise the national average, and it will result in a never-ending process. For this reason, average ratios are not a satisfactory measure of adequacy.

Since the major depression of the early 1930's, bank deposits have increased at a much faster rate than bank capital accounts. During this period, while deposits have increased about fourfold, capital accounts have merely doubled. There is a need for many banks to further strengthen their capital accounts, not only for the purpose of being able to absorb losses, but for the important function of being able to provide adequate credit.

There is some indication that banks realize the desirability of strengthening their capital funds to assets ratio and in the period from 1946 to 1961 this ratio on all insured commercial banks increased from 6.3% to 8.9%.

Capital accounts must be strengthened in times of prosperity and growth, not only to meet the increasing needs of growth, but to provide a bulwark of strength against periods of depression.

Although gross earnings of banks since World War II have been extremely high, increasing taxes have made it difficult to plow back earnings into capital at a rate sufficient to meet capital needs. This fact has caused an increasing number of banks to seek new capital through the sale of additional stock.

A growing, progressive bank should have a definite

plan and policy for meeting the needs for increased capital, and if sufficient earnings cannot be retained to meet the need, then a program for obtaining additional capital through the sale of stock, should be adopted. It is management's obligation to study such situations and have an appropriate plan for taking care of increasing capital requirements.

DIVIDENDS

As pointed out in the opening paragraph of this chapter, the second function of bank capital is to earn and pay an adequate return to its owners. The determination as to what is an adequate return to stockholders is not an easy question to decide, since a number of factors must be considered. As stated above, the primary purpose of capital must be to protect deposits. After deposits have been well protected through accumulation of adequate capital and surplus and all reasonably expected contingencies have been protected through adequate reserves, the stockholders have a right to expect a reasonable distribution of the bank's profits remaining in the undivided profits account. It is to be expected that dividend rates will vary from time to time as earnings fluctuate upward or downward. This is true of bank stocks just as other common stocks. It is a characteristic of bank earnings, however, that they do not tend to fluctuate as widely as industrial corporations according to whether times are good or bad. For this reason, bank dividends are more apt to be regular and stable than many other types of corporations. However, from the stockholders' viewpoint, there is no virtue in maintaining a steady rate of dividend if such a policy prevents stockholders from receiving a fair share of abnormal profits in the form of extra dividends in periods in which earnings justify it.

A sound policy in this respect would seem to prescribe the payment of a regular, semiannual dividend at the highest rate that the historical earnings record indicates may be probably maintained without interruption, with the expectation that at the end of the fiscal year, a portion of other available earnings (after all capital requirements, reserves, and contingencies have been met) will be distributed as an extra dividend.

In arriving at a dividend policy for a particular bank, the long term record of its earnings in good times and in depression years should be studied. Needs for increasing the capital structure should always receive priority over dividend distributions.

The Federal Revenue laws require that corporations shall distribute at least one half of the net earnings to stockholders as dividends unless there are sound reasons why the corporation should accumulate earnings. In recognition of the need for banks to conserve earnings for the purpose of strengthening capital, commercial banks are exempted from the provisions of the statute penalizing the accumulation of corporate earnings, nevertheless, many banks do follow the practice of distributing fifty per cent or more of the net earnings each year as dividends. Such a procedure may not be unsound if the bank's capital ratios are satisfactory, its assets are sound, the bank is enjoying good management, and the earnings record appears stable. There can be no acceptable "rule of thumb" that can be applied by bank management to determine a sound dividend policy. Each case must be studied with due regard to all of the factors involved. The executive officers should, through study and research, provide the directors with the facts and a recommendation. However, the dividend decisions must be made by the Board of Directors in the

light of what seems to be to the best interests of the bank's depositors, as well as its stockholders. Such decisions should be the result of mature deliberations, and not a product of hasty action.

The subject of stock dividends to bank shareholders has been the subject of some misunderstanding and "fuzzy thinking" on the part of both shareholders and bank management. It should be perfectly obvious to all concerned that a stock dividend to existing shareholders is simply a similar process to changing a ten dollar bill into a five dollar bill and five ones, or other appropriate denominations. Immediately following the stock dividend, the shareholder has nothing more than he had immediately before the dividend.

The benefits from a stock dividend normally result from the increased aggregate dividend distribution that usually follows a stock dividend, and the market phenomenon that frequently stimulates the market value of the divided shares to higher proportionate levels.

The increase of bank capitalization through the sale of additional shares is usually accompanied by option warrants to existing shareholders giving the shareholder the right to subscribe to additional shares at a stated price, and in a fixed proportion to shares then owned. The price at which the new stock is offered to old shareholders is usually at a figure somewhat less than the estimated price at which the public will be willing to purchase the new shares. This price differential should give the option warrants a market value that will permit the shareholder to sell the warrants if he does not wish to exercise the right to purchase additional stock.

While stock dividends and option warrants are usually enthusiastically received by shareholders, all concerned should fully realize that an increased number of shares and increased total capitalization that is not accompanied by proportionately increased earnings does not benefit the shareholders.

Banks contemplating the marketing of a sizable amount of additional stock frequently utilize the services of an investment dealer or a syndicate of investment dealers to provide an orderly market for the additional shares. The nature of the contract with the investment dealer or dealers, and the issuing bank will, of course, depend upon the local circumstances, and the estimated market demand for the additional shares to be offered.

Closely related to the adequacy of capital and surplus accounts is the matter of appropriate reserves for losses and contingencies. As pointed out in the beginning of this chapter, unallocated reserves for contingencies may be properly considered as part of the capital structure as contrasted to reserves for known liabilities such as taxes and accrued items of that nature. It is a matter of discretion as to whether such reserves are carried in undivided profits or set up in a special reserve account. There is some advantage in the latter method since a large undivided profits account often is a temptation toward a too liberal dividend policy. Adequate reserve accounts for contingencies is a constant reminder that such contingent liabilities do exist, and should be provided for.

The maintenance of adequate capital, surplus, undivided profits and reserve accounts, is a tremendously important function in the management of a bank. It is of far reaching importance to the depositors, the stockholders, the borrowers, and the community, and both the executive officers and the Board of Directors must fully understand

240

the principles involved and give the subject continuing attention.

For those who are interested in a further discussion of Bank Capitalization, an excellent discussion of this subject is contained in "The Problems of Adequate Bank Capital", an analysis prepared for the Illinois Bankers Association by Gaylord A. Freeman, Jr. Another thoughtful article on the subject of Bank Capital appeared in the April 1957 issue of *Banking*, the author being Ed Lyng, Associate Editor of *The Journal of Commerce*, New York City.

CHAPTER XXI

Bank Mergers and Consolidations

IN THE COURSE OF TIME, the management of nearly every bank is confronted with the question—is it desirable to merge or consolidate with another bank?

Sometimes the question arises from an approach made by representatives of another bank; again it may be presented to the management as a means of attaining certain desirable objectives that possibly can be most effectively achieved by merging with another bank.

Bank executives, therefore, should know something about the factors involved in mergers; some of the advantages that may be gained, some of the problems that are likely to be encountered, and the mathematical, or accounting calculations that will be involved in computing an equitable deal for the stockholders of the institutions involved in a merger.

The combination of separate banks into a single corporation may be accomplished either by the enlargement of an existing banking corporation or by the creation of a new corporation. If an existing corporation expands its capitalization and obtains the outstanding securities of another bank or banks by giving its own stock in exchange and then dissolves the other banking corporation, this is technically a "merger." However, if a new banking corporation is formed to acquire all of the assets of the banks involved, this process is known as a consolidation. The terms merger and consolidation are therefore frequently used interchangeably.

For the purposes of this chapter, all consolidations of two or more banks will be referred to as "mergers" regardless of whether such consolidations meet the legal or technical definitions of a merger.

Among the several ways in which banking institutions may be consolidated, or merged, are:

1. Forming a new corporation with a new name with stock in the new corporation being given in exchange to the stockholders of the merged banks in the proportion which their holdings in the old corporation bear to the aggregate assets of the merged institutions.

2. Increasing the capital stock of one of the merged banks by the aggregate value of the stock of the other bank or banks invoved in the merger, and exchanging the increased stock for the shares of the other bank or banks.

3. The purchase of all of the capital stock of a bank by another bank for cash with the purchased bank's being dissolved.

4. The purchase of all of the assets of a bank by another bank, with the liquidation of the liabilities of the purchased bank, and the dissolution of the selling corporation.

These are merely some of the routes that may be taken in combining the operations of two or more banks. There may be other combinations or variations of such procedures.

The form of consolidation that is preferable in a particular case is, to a considerable extent, a legal question to be decided in the light of whether the banks involved are national banks or state banks, and the agreed upon terms of consolidation. The attorneys for all banks concerned should participate in the consolidation agreement to make certain that all of the stockholders in all of the institutions will receive fair and equitable treatment.

It is a market phenomena that a merger or a merger rumor frequently results in an increased market price for the stock of the companies involved in the merger.

This is because mergers are sometimes regarded as an elixir or panacea that works magic on a business operation, but unfortunately this is not always true. The results of combined operations of two or more banks do not always produce the theoretical gains and profits which might have been anticipated and expected.

One of the first matters which deserves consideration in a proposed bank merger is determining the motivation for the suggested consolidation. What are the reasons why such a consolidation would be beneficial? The fact that a merger will result in a larger bank than either of the merged components is in itself no sound reason for a merger. To justify such a consolidation, there should be definite, specific objectives. Some of the most common motives may be listed as follows:

1. To obtain needed present executive ability.
2. To obtain executive material for future management.
3. To obtain skilled specialists in certain banking fields.
4. Inability to replace retiring management.

5. To obtain improved capitalization structure for one or more of the merged banks.

6. To improve a poor earnings record of one of the participating banks.

7. To form a bank of a larger size which will be more adequate to meet the needs of the trade area or the competition of other local banks.

8. To obtain larger loan limits.

9. To obtain or make possible more adequate banking quarters.

10. To obtain desirable branch bank locations or facilities.

11. To acquire or strengthen certain departments or services such as:
    (a) Trust Department
    (b) Foreign Department
    (c) Safe Deposit facilities
    (d) Travel Department

12. To obtain business of a type which one of the banks does not have, or accounts in a geographical area which one of the banks does not serve.

13. To obtain a better diversification of loans.

14. To obtain the benefits of a larger volume of business, with reduced overhead expenses. (It is to be noted that such benefits do not always result from a merger.)

15. To obtain potential tax advantages.

It is well recognized by bankers that no important business decision should ever be made without first considering the possible or probable tax effects, with particular emphasis on federal income taxes.

The relative importance of taxes as a motivation for mergers is probably not as great among banking corporations as when other types of business enterprises are involved. While it is difficult if not impossible to obtain authentic statistics with reference to the primary motivation for bank mergers, it is probable that tax motivations have not been a major factor in many bank mergers.

While there are other motives for mergers other than economic such as sociological or psychological motives, nevertheless in the vast majority of bank mergers the dominant motive is undoubtedly economic. The merger proposal should be critically scrutinized to make sure that the economic motive is for the benefit of all stockholders and not primarily for the benefit of management in the way of prestige, status, larger salaries, or better bonus or retirement provisions.

Offsetting some of the potential advantages mentioned above which might result from a merger, are a number of possible difficulties which should be duly weighed and considered.

Some of these possible disadvantages are:

1. Difficulties in acquainting the staff of the merged institutions with new associates, new policies, and new procedures.
2. The jealousies and internal competition and friction that frequently occur among the staff of merged banks.
3. Disposing of surplus people and surplus equipment that may result from the merger.
4. The problem of branches or other facilities which may not be needed after the merger, but which cannot be advantageously subleased or sold. ·
5. In some merger cases, new stationery, forms, signs, and so forth, will be required which will necessitate a waste of existing supplies and equipment.

6. The uncertainty of whether the proposed merger will be approved by the corporate supervisory authorities. (A further discussion of this subject is outlined below.)

7. The uncertainty as to how much of the existing business of the merged banks can be retained and whether any substantial part of the desirable business of any of the merged institutions will be lost as a by-product of the consolidation.

8. The likelihood that the resulting merged bank may be overstaffed in certain departments or positions, for instance, an unnecessary duplication of specialists such as purchasing agents, advertising director, personnel director, etc.

The attitude of the Federal and State supervisory authorities and the Federal Department of Justice toward bank mergers in recent years has undergone a decided change. In former years unless bank mergers produced virtually a monopoly in a given area, they were not frowned upon. Under the present prevailing philosophy, if the proposed consolidation will result in *materially lessened* competition, such proposed bank mergers will probably be denied by both the Department of Justice and the supervisory authorities. This change of policy with respect to bank mergers serves to restrict and curtail mergers that might otherwise be desirable.

Once it is decided that the advantages of a proposed merger apparently outweigh the probable disadvantages, it is necessary to prepare the terms of the merger. The financial terms of the proposed agreement will, in most cases, be the determining factor whether the proposal will be approved by the stockholders of the respective institutions.

In addition to the financial terms of the proposal, however, some other questions that may present difficulties are:

1. Who will be the Chief Executive of the merged banks, and what will be the relative rank and salary of the other officers?

2. Who will compose the Board of Directors of the merged banks?

3. If the policies of the component banks have not been identical, or similar, what policies will be followed in the merged banks?

4. Will all of the officers and employees of all of the component banks be retained, regardless of whether they are actually needed, and if so, for how long?

5. How will fringe benefits such as retirement plans, profit sharing plans, group insurance, etc., be equalized?

6. How will staff salaries be reconciled? (Usually salaries and benefits have to be increased to the level of whichever merged bank is highest.)

One of the most difficult problems that is presented in any proposed bank merger is to determine a mathematical formula or method of valuation for the financial terms of the merger that will be fair and equitable for all stockholders.

The valuation process is not one that can be reduced to a definite formula that can be followed in all cases. There are at least four principal methods of valuation that might be used or taken into consideration in the value determination involved in the process of a bank merger. Among the methods are:

1.   Book Value
2.   Appraisal Value
3.   Market Value
4.   Earnings Value

In most instances all of the four methods mentioned above will perhaps have some bearing on the merger value and seldom will one of the four values referred to be used as a trading basis to the exclusion of all others.

Seldom can book value be exclusively used for bank merger valuation purposes due to the lack of uniformity of accounting methods used by different banks. Book values also fail to register current values.

Appraisal values are apt to be considered as the most equitable basis for merger agreements but it must be recognized that an appraisal even by competent disinterested parties is only an expert opinion and qualified appraisers often fail to agree, since appraising is not an exact science. There is always the possibility that the appraised value will not be consistent with the earnings record of the appraised bank or its future potential earnings. While a current appraisal of assets is an important measure of a bank's value, it is not necessarily the final answer to the problem of valuation for the purposes of a proposed merger.

The market value of an entire banking corporation is difficult or impossible to determine. Market value by popular definition is an amount that would be agreed upon between a willing seller and a willing buyer. However, banks are not commonly sold *in toto*. Market value might be estimated as the aggregate market price of all of the outstanding shares, but such a valuation is questionable since the "over-the-counter" market price per share may not be reasonable if all of the outstanding shares or a substantial quantity is thrown on the market.

Even the rumor of a possible merger may change the "over-the-counter" market on a given bank stock to the extent that it will completely distort the aggregate market value of the outstanding shares.

The earnings value (both historical and potential) of a bank of course is entitled to considerable significance in a merger valuation. It is a fairly well accepted business maxim that "what a business is worth is determined by what it will earn." The stability of earnings over a long period of time is a strong factor in evaluating the ultimate worth of a given bank. Wide fluctuations in earnings which are not consistent with the earnings records of other well managed banks would serve to discount the earnings value of a bank. It is of course extremely difficult to project with any degree of accuracy the effect that a change in management resulting from a merger will have on future earnings of a merged bank.

The determination of a valuation for merger purposes should be a job for non-partisan certified public accountants, who are experienced in bank accounting. The process will likely require the adjustment of balance sheets in all banks included in the merger to reflect understated or overstated assets or liabilities. The judicious appraisal of some types of bank assets and liabilities is not an easy or simple matter. In a similar manner, the earnings and expense statements of the institutions should be adjusted over a period of several years so that they will reflect identical accounting principles and methods.

Only after such accounting adjustments have been completed can an evaluation be made on which to base an equitable trade between the institutions. Sometimes circumstances exist whereby it is to the advantage of one group to pay a premium to obtain a desired merger or perhaps one group will feel that the benefits from a proposed consolidation are such that the group will be willing to discount its holdings to achieve the desired result.

One of the characteristics of merger proposals and discussions is that an attempt is usually made to conduct the negotiations in a climate of secrecy to prevent speculation in the shares of the banks concerned, which might upset the delicate balances of valuation. As a practical matter it is very difficult and often impossible to prevent a leak of information or rumors of a proposed merger.

A critical question that should be asked and answered for each group of stockholders is: Will the proposed merger result in larger *pro rata* earnings for our shareholders?

This query is nearly always difficult to answer in advance, but unless the proposal seems to offer reasonable expectation of an affirmative answer within a few years, then the consolidation proposal should probably be answered in the negative, unless the terms can be altered to offer the prospect of investment improvement to all stockholders.

The final question to be answered by the Chief Executive of the banks involved in a proposed merger should be: Is this a proposal which I can conscientiously recommend to our stockholders with confidence that within a reasonable period the stockholders will have a better investment than they would have if the proposed merger is not consummated?

For further reading on the general subject of mergers and consolidations, the following references are suggested:

"Financial Organization and Management" by Charles W. Gerstenberg, published by Prentice-Hall, Inc.

"Corporation Finance" by Burtchett and Hicks, published by Harper & Bros.

"Financial Policies of Corporations" by A. S. Dewing, published by Ronald Press.

"Corporate Financial Policy" by Guthmann and Dongall, published by Prentice-Hall.

"Bank Mergers," New York Institute of Finance Bulletin No. 8, January 1962, published by New York University Graduate School of Business Administration.

CHAPTER XXII

The Bank President's Role

IN A DISCUSSION of the role or function of a bank president, it must be done with the realization that there can be no standardization. The role of the bank president must necessarily vary from bank to bank on account of the difference in organizational setups resulting from size, the extent to which the bank is departmentalized, the number of specialists in the various banking functions included on the staff, and the background of the president himself.

It is well known in banking circles that bank titles in themselves have little significance. The day-to-day duties of the presidents of any specific banks might vary widely in their nature. It is certain that the role of the bank president in a large city bank with 100 or more officers, will be quite different from the day-to-day duties of the president in a medium sized bank, or in a small bank with two or three officers.

In the very small bank, the president, as well as most of the bank staff, must necessarily be generalists, and be familiar with all phases of the bank's operations. In the larger banks, there is an increasing tendency for most of the officers to be specialists in certain areas of banking, and it is somewhat rare in a sizable bank to find an officer who is equally as well skilled in all of the major functions of banking, including investments, lending, and operations.

As indicated, a discussion in this area cannot very well deal with specifics, nor can it be dogmatic. In schools in the military services, it is frequently impressed upon the students that with reference to military tactical problems, there is never a specific solution, and the student is expected to provide "*an* approved solution," with emphasis upon the fact that such a solution cannot be considered *the* approved solution.

So it is with the role of the bank president. There are a number of general principles, ideas, and philosophies that may be applicable, but certainly no hard and fast rules of procedure or behavior can be strictly applied.

Perhaps the most important single factor in determining the role a particular bank president will occupy in his own bank, will be determined by his previous education and experience. Previous business experience is perhaps more dominant in this respect rather than the president's formal education.

Among medium sized banks, the largest number of bank presidents seem to be former lending officers. Occasionally we see a president who has been an investment specialist; once in a while the bank president's principal, previous experience has been largely in banking operations, and every now and then we find a bank president who is a former trust officer, but percentagewise, the largest number of commercial bank presidents seem to be former lending officers. It is virtually impossible for any one officer to have extended experience in each of the major functions in banking.

Sometimes we see a bank president who ascends to that position directly from the active practice of law, but the practice of law, unless it is followed by a considerable volume of banking experience, is not an ideal background for the presidency of a sizable bank. The president of a commercial bank, assuming that he is the chief executive officer, should be a generalist rather than a specialist. It is realistic to suppose that the well organized bank might have a specialist in each of the principal functions, who will be far wiser in those respective functions than the president of the bank. The president then becomes a co-ordinator, with a staff of specialists in each field with the president as the team captain, or quarterback, who calls the plays and directs the strategy which is designed to achieve the best team effort.

Monroe Kimbrel, Chairman of the Board of the First National Bank of Thomson, Georgia, and Vice President of the American Bankers Association, in a speech before the Louisiana Bankers Association in May, 1962, made the following statement:

"The banker of the future will not be the banker who knows everything and does everything connected with the successful operation of his bank. He will be the executive manager who knows where to get the information and specialized help he will need to operate successfully in a profit-motivated economy."

From the standpoint of profit and earnings, if any one function of a bank can be singled out as most important, it would probably be the conversion function, as discussed in Chapter X.

It is to be observed that in making the daily decisions,

255

the Conversion Committee of a commercial bank is primarily concerned with the immediate outlook rather than the long-term economic picture. Nevertheless, day-by-day decisions cannot entirely ignore trends, nor the significance of the long-term outlook. Neither the president nor any committee in a bank can apply any degree of knowledge or process of reasoning with the possible assurance that the future can be accurately forecast. About the best that can be expected in most cases is that the group will make an intelligent guess.

In daily decisions in both lending and in the purchase of securities, such decisions must be influenced by the economic situation. The economic situation at any given moment, of course, is a complex matter upon which no two individual people can completely agree in all aspects since it involves the international situation, both economic and military, the national economic scene with all of its political overtones, the state and regional economic climate, and even the purely local scene. An entirely clear picture is never presented. It is always complicated, and the situation at all levels, international, national, state, and local, is seldom what might be considered as "normal." Indeed there is perhaps no recognizable norm in the economic situation at any level. What might have been considered normal at one period may be abnormal on another date. History never repeats itself in exactly recurring patterns, and the banker who waits for normal conditions will probably never find them. We have a tendency to look back on certain periods and consider them as normal, but always the current situation seems to present complex problems which, at the moment, seem unusual and abnormal. The only state of normality seems to always embrace a group of complex and difficult problems.

Perhaps the goal that a bank president should seek to achieve with respect to economic information, is a broad understanding of the principles of economics, a general understanding of economic history as to what has happened in the past, and as complete an understanding as possible of the interpretation of current events, or what is happening at the moment, not only on the local scene, but in broader areas as well.

The nature of the relationship between the bank president and his customers is such that the customer expects the banker to be well versed in all matters affecting business conditions, and in a position to inform and advise the customer as to economic problems. The banker is in a favored position to exert considerable influence in his community by being well informed, and to use his position and knowledge to become a leader in the community.

A complete understanding of economics cannot ignore the field of government and politics (politics in this sense being defined as "pertaining to the conduct of government").

Having indicated the duties and responsibilities of a bank president to provide leadership in the field of economics, such responsibility being not only to the bank staff, but to the community at large, it seems appropriate to consider the ways and means through which the banker will inform himself in these areas. Bank executives, like all other business and professional men, have many demands made on their time, not only during business hours, but with many extracurricular activities as well. A part of the necessary equipment of the bank president should be a broad, general education, including a thorough understanding of the principles of economics. Coupled with this must be a more or less organized or systematic procedure for keeping up with daily events, and a search to interpret the meaning and effect of such events on the business of the bank and its customers. There is no shortage of material in this area. The real problem is for the banker to organize his time and to select the sources of information he will attempt to utilize. He will have definite need of many sources of information covering the various levels of activities, and the various types of investments with which he may be concerned. To a considerable extent, there will be an overlap between general economic information and specific investment data. There is no hard and fast line which separates one field from the other.

It is utterly impossible for a bank president, or anyone, to read all of the news and data which is available to provide him with current economic and investment information. It must necessarily be a selective process in which certain sources and publications will be considered a "must," and many others utilized to the extent that time and circumstances will permit.

No one can compile a prescription which will serve as an appropriate guide to all bank presidents for the current data that will enable them to successfully play the role which they are expected to fulfill in the field of economics and investments. It is possible, however, to give some suggestions, and perhaps set up an ideal target, realizing that it will not fit all cases, and admitting that its achievement would probably require more time than any individual will find available.

Of course certain financial periodicals might well be expected to be a "must" on every bank president's reading list. Leading the list would probably be *The Wall Street Journal*, with its broad, general coverage of economic, financial, and investment news at the international, national, regional, and state levels. Although much of the information contained in *The Wall Street Journal* can be gained from other sources, the fact that it is gathered and centralized in one publication while it is new, makes it a tool that can hardly be ignored. At one time, *The Wall Street Journal* was considered almost exclusively a periodical for bankers and financiers, but it is surprising today how many business and professional men are daily readers of *The Wall Street Journal* for the purpose of keeping up with the general business climate.

In addition to *The Wall Street Journal,* a bank president, even if he lives a considerable distance from New York, should probably subscribe to one of the New York City dailies in order to obtain the benefit of items which may not appear in *The Wall Street Journal.* Both *The New York Times* and *The Herald Tribune* are recommended for this purpose. The international coverage and editorials of both of these papers are excellent. *The American Banker,* a daily newspaper published in New York City, is also a prompt medium for learning of current spot news events which directly affect banking. Other publications of a general nature which will keep the banker well informed and alert on the international and national levels, are *U. S. World & News Report, Newsweek* and *Time* magazines.

In the trade journal field every banker should read *Banking,* the journal of the American Bankers Association. If your bank specializes in the business of any particular industry, the executives should regularly read the trade journals of those industries.

Of course it is not necessary to mention that any banker will certainly read thoroughly and carefully his own local newspapers in order that he may know what is going on in his own trade area, and will use and apply his general information in the light of the specific conditions that exist currently in the local area.

Another valuable source of information at the local level is the personal interview with local businessmen, farmers, and other customers and acquaintances. It is to be noted, however, that such information must be judiciously evaluated in the light of the person who furnished it. For instance, one particular merchant may tell you that business is terrible and that sales volume is very poor. This may be entirely true of this merchant's own business, but it may be due largely to his own ineptness and not to business conditions.

In recent years the market has been surfeited with innumerable news letters and supposedly confidential information in the form of weekly news reports. Most of these have a certain amount of value, but they should be read with the full realization that in many cases they are not authoritative, and may not be prudently used as an authentic guide. Som of the best known in this field are *Kiplinger's Weekly Letter*, *Pratt's Banking Newsletter*, and *Prudden's Digest*. There are others of a similar nature.

Bankers should use every possible source and means of acquiring investment information, but the decisions based on such information must be the banker's own decision, and cannot be the conclusions or decisions of others. Some bankers may have such complete confidence in certain investment dealers that it is their custom to phone the investment dealer and tell him they have a certain amount of money available for investment in tax-free securities, and request the dealer to select appropriate issues and maturities, and deliver the securities to a city correspondent for the country banker's account. Such a delegation of investment authority, no matter how competent and reliable the investment dealer might be, is a flagrant delegation of responsibility which no bank president can justify. All city banks which maintain an investment department are very happy to make investment recommendations to correspondents with respect to the selection of investments, but no investment officer of a bank should ever be willing to make such a decision that is inescapably fixed on the purchasing banker. Investment dealers, and city correspondents with investment departments, fulfill a very useful function, but the function definitely should not include the making of investment decisions for another bank.

Nearly every bank, regardless of how small it might be, usually has on its board of directors one or two men who have been successful in the management of their own affairs, and have acquired considerable information and experience in investment matters. The service of directors of this type on an investment committee to counsel and advise with the bank's executive officers in making investment decisions, can often provide a viewpoint that may be somewhat different from the traditional and conventional banker's viewpoint, and for this reason can be exceedingly helpful and valuable.

No bank president can completely fulfill his expected role in the bank unless he keeps in close touch with the local real estate situation. This is perhaps more nearly true in the smaller institutions than in the large metropolitan banks; however, banks of all sizes are apt to have a direct interest in the local real estate situation for many reasons. Most bankers in small and medium sized banks are engaged in real estate mortgage lending to some extent and, while the bank president may not personally handle real estate loans, he should be thoroughly familiar with the trade territory served by his bank, and have first hand knowledge of all real estate developments. Such knowledge can probably be best obtained by getting out of the bank frequently and traveling through the territory and neighborhoods which the bank serves. It will probably be another one of those duties for which it is exceedingly hard to find appropriate time, but it is probably the only manner in which the bank president can keep fully informed and obtain a clear picture with reference to the development that is taking place in his area.

It is not possible to summarize in a few sentences the role of the typical bank president in an average bank. In the first place, there is no such thing as a typical bank president and probably no such thing as an average bank.

The president's role will vary widely with the size of the bank. In the smaller bank the president usually fills the role of the department head in all of the major functions. In the medium sized banks in the lower brackets, a president is apt to serve as department head of at least one major function, such lending or investments, or maybe both.

Of course the larger banks will have specialists as department heads for all of the principal functions and perhaps at least one full-time economist as well.

But regardless of the number of specialists on the bank staff in the field of investments and economics, these two closely related fields are areas in which the bank president in banks of any size must be well informed, and must constantly keep up to date.

CHAPTER XXIII

The Board of Directors

THE DESIRABLE QUALIFICATIONS for the director of a bank fall into at least two broad categories —that is, legal and necessary qualifications, and desirable, personal qualifications. The legal requirements for the director of a national bank are similar to (though not exactly in accordance with) the requirements for a State bank in most jurisdictions. Both require a certain minimum amount of the bank's stock to be owned outright by the director free from any encumbrances or pledges. The director of a national bank is required to own not less than $1,000 of the par value stock of his bank. In some states the required stock for the directors of a state bank are somewhat less.

There is a requirement that the directors of a national bank must reside in the state in which the bank is located or within 100 miles of the area served. There is also a prohibition of an individual serving as a member of a board of directors of banks which are in competition with each other. Securities dealers are not eligible as bank directors for the obvious reason that it would be unethical for them to buy from or sell securities to the bank which they are serving. There appear to be no mandatory requirements for regularity of attendance of directors at board meetings, however, the national bank examiners carefully scrutinize the attendance of directors at board meetings and make a report of such attendance on the occasion of each examination.

PERSONAL QUALIFICATIONS

In addition to the legal qualifications mentioned above, there are many different personal qualifications which are desirable for bank directors. The most impor-, tant qualification, perhaps, is of a general nature, and is the ability to contribute something constructive to the management of the bank. One qualification that should be considered a "must" is the reputation for integrity and respectability. In no other business, perhaps, is integrity and the command of confidence more necessary than in banking. There is no place in the organziation of a bank, at any level, for persons of doubtful, or dubious reputation. Alertness and good business judgment should also come high on the list, also a knowledge of and participation in community affairs. One element of evidence as to the suitability of an individual for a position on a bank's board of directors, is a demonstration of the fact that the individual has enjoyed success in his own right in whatever profession or field of business that he pursues. Whether a person happens to be wealthy is not, in itself, convincing unless the person has demonstrated good business and investment judgment, and the ability to conserve and manage his wealth if he has inherited it and not created it.

In some instances banks have chosen directors largely

on the basis of their ability to obtain and control banking business. While this is certainly a desirable quality in any director, it should not be the principal requirement, and an individual who does not measure up in other respects as desirable, should not be included on a bank's board of directors merely because he is believed to be a business-getter. A bank should have the right to expect the confidence and patronage of its directors, but it is unwise to attempt to buy banking business through the bestowal of directorships.

IMPORTANCE OF BALANCE

As to the board of directors collectively, it is very important to have "balance" on the board—balance in ages so that the board will have some seasoned veterans with long experience, and a sufficient number of younger, vigorous men, receptive to new ideas, who will have many useful years of active business life ahead of them. Also, balance as to occupations, so that the viewpoint of different industries, businesses, and professions will be represented. It is also important to have balance on the board as to residence and social groups so that the entire board will not come from the same "clique."

The president of a bank is necessarily a member of the board of directors, and in the medium sized and larger banks, it is customary for one or two additional, full-time officers of the bank to serve on the board of directors. However, it is desirable that the majority of the Board be "outside" directors rather than full-time officers of the bank. A board composed entirely of bank officers, whose primary interest and knowledge of business are centered in banking, would not be a well balanced board, and would not serve the broad, useful purpose that a well diversified board can offer. Even where the stock of a bank might be held or controlled by one man, or his family, it is definitely desirable not to have a "rubber stamp" board which merely follows the will and direction of the majority stockholder. Such a board does not fulfill the real purpose for which it is intended.

Since law and custom impose stern responsibilities upon bank directors, it is pertinent to inquire into the motives that impel persons to accept bank directorships. In some cases, the ownership of a considerable amount of stock and the desire to see the bank prosper for the purpose of dividends and stock enhancement, is the motivation for seeking, or accepting a bank directorship. But among medium sized and larger banks this is probably not the primary motivation of most of the directors. It appears that personal financial gain is not usually the principal reason for accepting bank directorships. The directors' fees are seldom large enough to fully compensate the director for the time and responsibility required. It is to the credit of the directors of the banks of America that the money motive is not their prime consideration. Prestige, and a desire to serve the community are probably the principal reasons why people are willing to be bank directors.

DIRECTORS SHOULD DIRECT

Perhaps the most uncertain feature with respect to bank directors is the degree with which the board shall actually direct or manage the corporation. The laws under which banks and other corporations are organized, provide that the corporation shall be managed by its board of directors, yet the manner, and the extent of the directors' influence in managing the corporation is not specified. The usual interpretation of the directors' obligation and authority recognizes that the day by day handling of operations must necessarily be delegated by the directors to executive officers of the corporation. Under this theory, a board of directors should determine broad, general policies, and "direct", but should not attempt to manage. One text-book on the subject has stated it this way—"Let the directors 'direct' and management 'manage'."

It is obviously impractical in any but the smallest banks for outside directors to make decisions on individual cases. They should not be expected to have the experience and skill to tell the executive officers of the bank how to do their jobs in detail. Outside directors should not be expected to be "super-bankers" or a Supreme Court which "second guesses" the management to the extent that the executive officers are handicapped in their daily duties. In some cases, the outside directors, even though they are highly skilled in their own business or profession, actually may not have a thorough knowledge of banking principles, and may be poorly qualified to make executive decisions for the bank.

Perhaps the most important duty and obligation of a corporation's board of directors, is to choose capable executive and operating officers, and maintain a continuous appraisal of their effectiveness.

In stating that the directors should "direct" and the management "manage," it is not to be implied that the board of directors should merely be a group of "yesmen" who will be rubber stamps and approve any suggestions or policies that management provides. It is important that every board of directors of a bank should have a clearcut understanding of its proper and appropriate functions, and discharge those functions to the best of its ability without attempting to invade the prerogatives and func-

267

tions which the executive officers should be best equipped to handle.

ROLE SHOULD NOT BE PASSIVE

The role of the bank director should not be a passive one in which the director merely attends occasional meetings and votes "yes" or "no" on motions proposed to the board. There are many definite, constructive helps that directors, individually and collectively can give to aid bank management. As suggested above, the constant and continuing valuation of the effectiveness of the bank's staff should be a primary duty of the Board; also a familiarity with the operating results, and the ability to interpret whether these results are good, bad, or mediocre.

It is generally recognized that the determination of broad, general policies, such as the bank's loan policies and investment policies, is the function of the board of directors. While most banks would readily agree to this theory in comparatively few banks has the board of directors accepted the responsibility fully by clearly enunciating the loan and investment policies, and reduced them to writing. Unless such policies are written, it is not likely that there will be a clear understanding by all concerned as to such policies, nor that they can be satisfactorily maintained, or that they will be changed from time to time to meet new circumstances.

Assuming that the board has met its obligation, and has adopted policies, whether they are reduced to writing or not, it is certainly the obligation of every board member to be familiar with these policies, and to be reasonably certain that they are followed, kept up-to-date, and changed when necessary or desirable.

Another constructive service that may be rendered by directors, is to maintain an objective observation of the service rendered by the bank to the customer. Most bank directors are customers of the bank, and therefore should be in a position to watch carefully the manner in which its services are performed, realizing that a special effort is probably being made to serve a director well. Certainly, if a director does not receive courteous, efficient, satisfactory service, it is reasonable to suppose other customers are receiving even poorer service.

In the same manner that directors might critically observe the bank's services, it is also desirable that they should objectively evaluate the bank's public relations and advertising program, and inform the management if and when such program does not seem to be effective from the viewpoint of an outsider.

AUDIT PROGRAM

A bank's board of directors should realize that the periodical examinations by a supervisory agency does not constitute a thorough audit of a bank, and the directors should insist upon an adequate audit program either in the form of a continuous internal audit by personnel competent to conduct such a program, or upon an independent audit by public accountants. In many situations, both an internal audit program, and periodical audits by outside, independent accountants are justified but the audit program is not complete unless the directors assume the responsibility of carefully examining and appraising the auditor's reports to see if corrective action is needed, and the same responsibility is true toward the reports of bank examiners.

Bank directors are usually men of affairs who are widely acquainted and have above-average knowledge in some areas. Directors may be able, from time to time, to provide information to the bank which can lead to new business or may be of assistance in reaching credit decisions. Such assistance from directors should not be too much to expect.

There is no standardization among banks in the amount and character of information that is furnished by management to directors nor the manner and form in which it is presented.

INFORMATION FOR DIRECTORS

The minimum of information that should be provided directors is a monthly financial statement consisting of a balance sheet and an income and expense statement, together with a report of loans made and investments purchased and sold. Instead of making such reports orally at the board's monthly meeting, there are a number of advantages in giving the directors written reports which they can more easily assimilate and remember.

One satisfactory plan for directors' monthly reports is to provide each director with a ring-binder which is placed on the table in the directors' room an hour before the scheduled monthly directors' meeting. This book may contain the following reports and statistics:

1. Comparative balance sheets.
2. Comparative income report.
3. Comparative expense report.
4. Statement of securities purchased, sold and matured.
5. A report of large loans consummated.
6. A report of delinquent loans with an estimate of probable losses.

Banks that maintain income and expense budgets will undoubtedly find that the directors will be interested, from time to time, to learn how closely the actual operating figures approximate the budget estimates, and it is desirable to make quarterly or semi-annually reports to the board with reference to the status of the bank budget, with explanations for any items which represent a material variance from the original estimates.

Banks which are members of the Federal Reserve system receive annually, comparative ratios prepared by the Federal Reserve Bank for various deposit groups. Through the means of these ratios, it is possible for a bank to see how its various items of income and expense compare with other banks of approximately the same deposit size in the Federal Reserve District. Such comparative reports should be carefully analyzed, and attempts made to explain or rationalize any items which appear to be out of line with similar items for other banks. Such analytical reports should be furnished to the board of directors, regardless of whether the comparison is favorable, or otherwise, since if it is unfavorable, it should be the responsibility of the board to determine the cause and seek appropriate remedies.

Management, from time to time, will also find other comparative statistics available which will be of interest to the directors and it is management's obligation to keep the board fully informed in this respect.

Of course the board of directors will receive the annual statement which goes to all stockholders, but management should feel obligated to furnish the board an even more detailed analysis of the annual report than is customarily given to the stockholders.

COMMITTEES

The board of directors of a bank usually has several

committees composed of directors, which perform functions which cannot conveniently be handled by the entire board. The committees most commonly found are—an executive committee; an examining committee; a loan committee (frequently called the "discount" or "finance" committee); an investment committee; a salary committee; and a trust committee, or trust investment committee, if the bank operates a trust department. The names of these committees are usually self-explanatory.

The executive committee is a group which is usually authorized to act for the board in the interim between the regular monthly meetings of the board. An examining committee is required in all national banks, and the duties of the examining committee are fixed by banking regulations, including the requirement that the directors make, or cause to be made, an examination of the bank at least once each year. In practically all banks except the smallest, the directors' examining committee delegates the conduct of the required examination to an independent accountant who reports to the committee.

The directors' loan committee (by whatever name known), performs the function of scrutinizing the loans made by the banks' officers, and usually approves the larger lines of new credit. Since it is impractical for the entire board to discharge the directors' responsibility for supervising loans, the directors' loan committee, through frequent meetings, can give the loans much closer supervision than if the loan reports are submitted to the entire board at the regular monthly meetings. It is customary for the minutes of the directors' loan committee to be presented to, and approved by the entire board at the regular monthly meetings.

The directors' investment committee serves in a manner similar to the directors' loan committee in that it meets periodically to review and approve purchases and sales of bank investments.

In most banks, the salaries of employees below officer level, are determined by the executive officers of the bank, but the officers' salaries are fixed annually by the board of directors. It is customary for a committee of directors to meet prior to the board's annual meeting and discuss the officers' salary situation with the executive officers of the bank, and prepare a schedule of officers' salaries for the ensuing year, which is presented to the board at the annual meeting. In some banks, the directors' salary committee confers periodically with the executive officers of the bank concerning the general salary schedule of the staff below the officer level.

Every national bank exercising trust powers is required to maintain a committee known as the trust committee, or trust investment committee, which must perform certain duties as provided in Regulation F of the Federal Reserve Board. These duties include the approval of the acceptance and termination of all trust accounts, the review of all assets in every trust account at least once each year, the approval of the purchase and sale of any trust assets, and the general supervision of the policies of the trust department.

It is highly desirable for the bank to maintain full and complete minutes of all directors' committee meetings.

LIABILITY OF DIRECTORS

On the subject of the liability of bank directors, some books have over-stressed the subject of potential liability. While such liability is real and the possibility exists, as a practical matter very few bank directors are ever confronted with actual civil or criminal liability for their actions as directors. The cases where directors have been assessed with liability are mostly cases involving fraud or dishonesty and sometimes gross negligence.

With respect to national banks, the United States Statutes provide as follows:

"If the directors of a national banking association shall knowingly violate, or knowingly permit any of the officers, agents or servants of the association to violate any of the provisions of this title, all the rights, privileges, and franchises of the association shall be thereby forfeited. And in cases of such violation every director who participated in or assented to the same shall be held liable in his personal and individual capacity for all damages which the association, its shareholders, or any other person shall have sustained in consequence of such violation."

Specific illustrations where directors have been held liable for illegal acts include:

a. Permitting loans to be made, secured by the bank's own stock.
b. Approving loans to borrowers in excess of the legal limit.
c. Receiving a fee for approving a loan.
d. Unlawful increase of capital stock.
e. Insufficient surety bonds.
f. Loans of trust funds to directors.
g. Approving *ultra vires* acts.
h. Permitting of extravagant or improvident expenditures in the conduct of the bank's affairs.
i. Authorizing improvident investments.

Clarence G. McDavitt, Jr., late president of the Somerville National Bank of Somerville, Massachusetts, in his book entitled "If You're a Bank Director"* has a chapter entitled "38 Ways to Get into Trouble." This chapter enumerates 38 specific ways that directors may violate banking laws that may result in criminal or civil liability.

The next chapter of McDavitt's book is entitled "Three Ways to Stay Out of Trouble." The three ways that he suggests are to study and analyze:

1. Examiners' reports.
2. Auditors' reports.
3. Directors' reports.

Treasury Department Form 1417, a 31 page booklet entitled "Duties and Liabilities of Directors of National Banks" is an official publication of the office of the Comptroller of the Currency for the guidance of national banks. Even though the publication is official in nature, it stresses the negative, or liability side more than the positive or constructive side of directors' activities.

REASONABLE DILIGENCE AND PRUDENCE

A bank director who uses reasonable diligence and uses the same degree of prudence in the bank's affairs that he exercises in his own business, need not fear liability for his acts as a director. But the degree with which a bank director's potential liability is stressed in some articles is enough to make any one extremely dubious about accepting a bank directorship.

Bank directors' meetings are normally presided over by the chairman of the board, or the president. The manner in which the meeting is conducted can add greatly to its effectiveness and to the amount of information that can

---

* Published by Bankers Publishing Company, 89 Beach St., Boston 11, Mass.

be conveyed and the volume of business dispatched.

Under the head of "Reports to Directors" it has been suggested that the monthly statistical report from management to the board be placed in ring binder notebooks which may be available in the directors' room before the time scheduled for the meeting. This will enable directors to study the figures prior to the meeting and be prepared to ask questions on any items on which further information is desired. This previous study of the reports should expedite the conduct of the meeting. The executive officers should be prepared to comment on any items which appear in the report which are unusual or particularly significant.

If the presiding officer prepares a typewritten agenda prior to the meeting and gives each director a copy, it will enable the board members to see what is scheduled for discussion and will enable the chairman to keep discussions limited to the matter then under consideration.

While there is no need for a bank board meeting to be excessively formal, it is desirable for it to proceed along orderly lines, with questions being presented on motions and votes taken in usual parliamentary procedure. Though it may not be necessary or desirable to strictly follow all of the formality of Robert's Rules of Order, some degree of formal procedure is desirable, and a time saver.

UNANIMOUS CONSENT NOT NECESSARY

Small boards sometimes get into the habit of seeking unanimous consent on all controversial questions, and failing unanimous approval, action is postponed. Such a practice is dangerous in that it amounts to giving each director an absolute veto which might result in a stalemate situation. An honest difference of opinion among bank directors can be a sign of active, healthy interest in the bank's affairs and after such differences of opinion have been freely expressed, the views of the majority should prevail. A board that merely rubber stamps, or "yesses" any proposal that is presented, is not fulfilling its real purpose.

In presenting matters for decision, the presiding officer should make certain that the scope of the motion is clearly stated and understood.

The minutes of the board of directors should be recorded in detail and it is often desirable to state the facts or reasoning upon which decisions are based. Such records may be useful if the legality of the action, or good faith of the board is challenged at a later date.

The minutes of each meeting should be read in full and approved at the next meeting and should never be dispensed with as is the custom in some organizations, because it is important that the board approve the manner in which its decisions have been expressed.

DIVIDEND POLICY

One of the more important duties of a bank's directorate is the supervision of its corporate financial structure and the dividend policy. Such decisions presuppose a thorough knowledge of the economics of corporation finance and every bank director has the duty of informing himself concerning the fundamental principles of bank capitalization and the functions of the various components of the capital structure.

There is apt to be a conflict of purpose between the executive management of a bank and some of the directors and stockholders in the application and use of earnings. Traditionally, management seeks to retain out of earnings sufficient funds for working capital, capital improvements, expansion, maintenance, and reserves for contingencies that occur. Stockholders, on the other hand, are apt to be primarily interested in the distribution of substantially all of the earnings as dividends. The board of directors must understand the viewpoints of both management and stockholders and maintain a proper balance between retaining earnings for needed purposes, and the payment of reasonable dividends.

In making decisions with respect to dividends, the directors must realize that they have duties toward other groups such as the depositors in providing adequate capital structure, the management in providing for needed maintenance and expansion, and to the other stockholders who are not on the board. Dividend decisions should not merely represent the selfish purposes of the board members, as opposed to the stockholders at large.

In recent years women have become increasingly important in the ·operation of banks. The proportion of women bank employees and women bank stockholders has increased steadily and women bank officers are no longer a novelty. No figures are available as to the number of bank directors in America who are women, but it is undoubtedly small, percentage-wise. There seem to be no very convincing arguments, either for or against women as directors of a bank. The only sound basis for such a decision is whether the woman proposed for the board possesses qualifications that will aid the bank.

DIRECTORS FEES

It is customary in banks as in most other corporations, to pay directors a fee for attendance at directors' meetings and for directors' committee meetings. The amount of such fees is usually provided in the bank by-laws and the normal range is from about $10 a meeting in the smaller banks, to $100 in the large, metropolitan banks, with the fees in the majority of banks ranging in the middle brackets between these figures. In most banks, full-time officers of the bank, who are on the board, do not receive directors' fees on the theory that the bank has paid for their participation through salary. Other banks reason that the officer's salary does not compensate him for the additional responsibility and potential liability of a board member and therefore allow officers the same fees as other directors. Some banks allow officer-directors fees for regularly scheduled directors' meetings, but no fees for special, called meetings or committee meetings.

The Board of Directors of every bank should have a clearly recognized and stated policy with reference to loans to directors or loans to corporations in which a director is financially interested. The bank examiners usually take special cognizance of such loans by listing them, even if they are not criticized or classified as to quality.

To decline to make sound loans to directors would deprive the bank of good potential business and place a further burden on the incentives of serving as a director. On the other hand, a director should fully recognize his responsibility to the bank's stockholders and not expect favored treatment and special rates. Some banks have adopted a policy that no loans shall be made to directors unless they are fully secured by acceptable collateral. Other banks require that all loans to directors shall be approved in advance by a majority of the board of directors.

LOANS TO DIRECTORS

Perhaps the soundest policy with respect to loans to directors is the pronouncement that such loans must in all respects conform to the same high standards expected of all other loans, and that the requirements of such loans must be no less rigid, but on the other hand, no more strict than for other loans. The same impartial treatment should apply on interest rates to directors.

It is fairly common for the bank's attorney or general counsel to be a member of the board of directors, yet McDavitt, in his book mentioned above, recommends that no directors should provide professional personal service to the bank for which he receives a fee or commission. This policy is not only intended to include lawyers, but accountants and appraisers. The reasoning behind this recommended policy is that in the fixing of fees and charges, it involves an adverse interest and the executive officers of the bank are at a disadvantage in such trans-actions with board members. Nevertheless, the majority of banks do have their attorneys and others doing business with the bank on the board, and it does not seem to occasion any great difficulty. Perhaps a good solution to such a problem, if it occurs, is to have any such fees and charges of a board member negotiated by a committee of the board rather than by the executive officers.

A rather delicate subject with reference to directors, and one on which very little reference material is available, is compulsory retirement of directors. It must be recog-nized that in theory at least, directors serve as representa-tives of stockholders and stockholders owning the required shares may name representatives on the board regardless of policies which the Board may establish as to age quali-fications and retirement. More often than not, however, the board controls enough shares of proxies to determine the personnel of the Board and to enforce a retirement policy if it is desirable to do so.

In the booklet published by The American Bankers Association entitled "A Bank Director's Job," the final section is devoted to the subject of Directors' retirement. The first point noted is that banks should recognize the existence of the problem and adopt a policy with reference to it. The following is quoted from that article:

RETIREMENT POLICY

"When is a director too old? To this question, there is no simple answer. Chronological age is one thing. Physiological age is another. Mental age is another. It would not be practicable to require directors to take an annual medical or intelligence test. Besides, many useful directors might not pass such a test. Some persons at 65 are older, by any criterion than others are at 75. If a bank's directors are to be retired when they become super-annuated, some arbitrary standard of superannuation must be adopted. Business, including banking, recognizes this fact with regard to officers and employees subject, some-times, to exceptions. Adoption of a normal retirement age makes possible graceful separation from power and respon-sibility in the case of officers and employees. The same principle has applicability to bank directors, and is being so applied.

"The chronological standard of retirement may not be the perfect solution, but it is at least impartial and avoids any suspicion of discrimination. It is impersonal and objective, preserving the individual's dignity without per-sonal implication."

Studies on the subject of the retirement of bank direc-tors have been made by the Connecticut Bankers Associa-tion, the Harris Bank & Trust Company of Chicago, The Lincoln-Rochester Trust Company of Rochester, N.Y., the

Holyoke Savings Bank of Holyoke, Massachusetts, and others.

Some of the conclusions reached by these studies are as follows:

1. A bank may select whatever standard it wishes as to retirement age for directors, but the important thing would seem to be that some standard be adopted.

2. No individual can possibly be a competent judge as to his own appropriate retirement age.

3. The existence of a policy or a standard obviates the necessity of an individual or a committee having to perform the unpleasant duty of informing a fellow-director that his retirement from the board is desirable.

4. A defined policy of retirement of directors makes it possible for a bank to conduct a more thorough search for new directors than is normally possible when vacancies on the board occur only in sporadic fashion as the result of death.

5. Honorary or advisory status for retired directors has certain advantages for both the bank and the retired director.

Among the advantages to the retired directors:

(a) The policy continues to endow them with the prestige associated with bank directorships.

(b) They may continue worth while social relations and friendships with their associates on the board and make new friends among younger leaders as they are elected to the board.

(c) The policy relieves retired directors of direct responsibility and liability since they no longer make decisions by voting upon them.

(d) As emeritus directors they may continue to keep in touch with the financial affairs in the community.

The Lincoln-Rochester Trust Company reports with reference to the reactions of retired directors—"They have been pleased with the plan in operation, stating that they enjoyed the contacts and privileges of being closely associated with the board of directors, sitting in on all deliberations, and being given an opportunity to voice their opinions, all without having to assume any of the responsibilities."

In summary, the duties of bank directors fall into four general categories—

1.   To choose and maintain a constant appraisal of the officers who operate the bank.

2.   To determine the policies which will regulate the manner in which the business of the bank is conducted.

3.   To observe, and insist upon the observation by all others, the laws under which the bank is organized.

4.   To preserve a sound corporate structure and to determine what dividends, if any, may be properly paid.

Those are the bare legal requirements of a bank director, but it is evident that they embrace a great responsibility to the bank, to the community, and to the nation.

Epilogue

A PROMINENT CLERGYMAN, who is a successful business administrator as well as a spiritual leader, has offered the following formula for successful administration:

Analyze
Organize
Deputize
Supervise

This simple management formula can well be adopted as the program for the chief executive of a medium sized bank.

The first step of the bank executive should be to analyze and fully understand the bank's business and its problems. This is of course not a one time job, but a continuing day-by-day function. The executive must analyze and interpret the daily, monthly, and other periodic reports, as well as the problems which are certain to arise.

Having analyzed and gained a clear comprehension of the bank's condition and its problems, the executive must determine what is to be done, and who is to do it. One

285

means of designating and delegating responsibilities to sub-ordinates, is an organization chart as described in Chapter I. Whether such charts are used or not the chief executive must use some effective form of communication to allocate duties and responsibilities to his staff. This process of organizing and assigning the bank staff to perform the various functions is an essential and important part of top management's responsibility.

There are distinct limits to the area of primary responsibility that any individual can effectively assume, regardless of his talents and capabilities. The executive who can effectively deputize specific responsibilities to others, thereby increases the sphere of his own usefulness. The "one man bank" must necessarily be limited to the very small institution that is not departmentalized. As long as the chief executive attempts to run a "one man bank" without deputizing responsibilities to others, the bank in question is almost certain to remain a small bank.

It is axiomatic that deputizing responsibilities to others necessitates granting authority to carry out those responsibilities, for responsibility without authority is an untenable situation.

Unfortunately, the deputizing of duties and responsibilities to others does not completely fulfill the function of the chief executive. Constant supervision and counseling is required of the chief executive to determine to what extent and to what degree the deputized duties, functions, and responsibilities are being carried out.

Perhaps the most important point that can be stressed with reference to the principal executive officer of a medium sized bank, is that he should be an over-all coordinator of all functions rather than the head of several departments. He must have intimate knowledge of what is going on in all departments, but should have some responsible supervisor in each department who can be depended upon to carry out policies and directions with reference to the department and keep the chief executive informed with reference to it.

In the typical medium sized bank the three major departments are Operations, Lending, and Investments, and sometimes a Trust Department or a Foreign Department may be a major department. Of course public relations and the audit function are important too, but they are corollary functions rather than primary.

The chief executive must have definite policies, objectives and plans for all departments and by frequent personal inquiry and observation must personally know the status of each department. A considerable portion of his time should be spent in the careful interpretation and analysis of the periodical detailed figures from the several departments. The figures and records for the current period should be carefully compared with similar records for previous periods in order to detect trends and forecast future developments.

The history of the past is most useful as a guide to the future and the chief executive of a bank must use the available statistics to plan for the future rather than wait for situations to develop which demand immediate planning and execution.

The chief executive of a medium sized bank will have a wide variety of duties ranging from abstract problems in high finance to very mundane affairs dealing with the simple and sometimes sordid personal problems of obscure people. A single day's diary would reveal a kaleidoscope of events, many entirely unrelated, which demand prompt and immediate attention and decision. One of his biggest problems will probably be the organization of his time so as to not permit the thousand little things that are thrust at him to prevent him from seeing clearly the "big picture" and from finding time to carry forward the overall program.

Appendix

A SUGGESTED RESOLUTION for a hypothetical, medium sized bank stating its lending policies as suggested in Chapter VII is outlined below, merely as an example:

BE IT RESOLVED, that the officers of this bank, in making loans and extending lines of credit, shall be guided by the following principles:

1. The management of the bank believes that sound local loans are one of the most satisfactory and profitable means of employing the bank's funds available for investment, and the bank, therefore, desires to make all of the sound loans that its resources permit and opportunity affords. The Board of Directors recognizes that the lending of money by commercial banks is a business that necessarily includes some business risks and the management of the bank is willing to undertake such reasonable risks. Some losses are to be expected in any lending program and a reserve of one-half of one per cent of the face amount of loans outstanding will be maintained as a reserve for loan losses.

2. The bank will not content itself with merely accepting and consummating all sound loans that are offered to the bank, but will aggressively seek to develop desirable loans of the types hereinafter described.

3. The lending activities of this bank will be under the general supervision of the Vice President in charge of loans, who will follow the policies and principles set forth in this resolution. The Vice President in charge of loans shall seek the advice and counsel of the President of the bank when in doubt as to credit decisions or questions involving the interpretation or application of loan policies.

4. All loans or lines of credit in the amount of $200,000 or more shall be approved in advance by the Directors' Loan Committee.

5. All loans in excess of the limits hereinafter provided for the various lending officers but less than $200,000, shall be approved in advance by the Officers' Loan Committee which shall be composed of the President, the Vice President in charge of loans, and one other lending officer designated by the President. In the event any member of the said committee is not available, any two members shall constitute a quorum.

6. The officers of the bank shall have authority to make loans up to the amount indicated by their respective names, without the approval of any committee, provided such loans are in accordance with the policies and principles herein expressed. Loans to any person, firm, or corporation in excess of the limits indicated, must be approved by the Officers' Loan Committee, or the Directors' Loan Committee, as hereinabove provided:

	Unsecured	Secured
John Q. Adams, President	$200,000.00	$200,000.00
John Doe, Vice President	200,000.00	200,000.00
Richard Roe, Vice President	25,000.00	50,000.00
John F. Jones, Asst. Vice Pres.	15,000.00	25,000.00
James Smith, Asst. Vice Pres. ..	10,000.00	25,000.00
Paul Davis, Asst. Cashier	5,000.00	15,000.00
Charles Clark, Asst. Cashier	2,500.00	5,000.00

7. Loans of the following types are considered desirable by this bank, provided each such loan meets the tests of a sound, prudent loan:

a. Loans to business concerns on a short-term basis, against a satisfactory balance sheet and earnings statement, usually for a term of not more than ninety days.

b. Loans to business concerns secured by a chattel mortgage on marketable business equipment. Such loans to be amortized over a period of not more than eighteen months.

c. Loans to wholesale companies against assignments of accounts receivable on a notification basis. The creditor's remittances in their original form on such loans should be delivered to the bank for credit to the borrower's loan.

d. Loans collaterally secured by negotiable U. S. Government bonds, such loans to be not more than 90% of the market value of the bonds.

Loans collaterally secured by securities listed on a recognized exchange, such loans to be not more than 75% of the market value of the collateral, and the loan must comply in all respects with Regulation "U" of the Federal Reserve System.

Loans, collaterally secured by unlisted securities which have a ready "over-the-counter" market; such loans should not be in excess of fifty per cent of the market value of the collateral.

e. Loans against the cash surrender value of life insurance; such loans should not exceed the cash surrender value less one year's premium.

f. Loans secured by the assignment of savings accounts in this bank.

g. Real estate loans may be made, secured by first liens on improved real estate, including improved farm land and improved business and residential properties. A loan secured by real estate shall be in the form of an obligation or obligations secured by mortgage. The amount of any such loan shall not exceed 50% of the appraised value of the real estate offered as security and no such loan shall be made for a longer term than five years except that:

1. Any such loan may be made in an amount not to exceed 66 2/3 per centum of the appraised value of the real estate offered as security, and for a term not longer than ten years if the loan is secured by an amortized mortgage under the terms of which the installment payments are sufficient to amortize 40 per centum or more of the principal of the loan within a period of not more than ten years; and

2. The foregoing limitations shall not apply to real estate loans which are insured under the provisions of Title II and Title VI of the National Housing Act.*

h. Real estate appraisals upon which mortgage loans are based shall be made by appraisers who are approved by the Directors' Loan Committee. Regardless of the value of the security, real estate mortgage loans shall not be made to borrowers who do not have a satisfactory credit record

---

* Section 24 of the Federal Reserve Act.

nor in cases where it appears likely that the property may have to be liquidated to satisfy the debt.

i. Unsecured personal loans to persons of good character with an assured income and satisfactory credit records when the purpose of such loan will be of ultimate benefit to the borrower. Such loans to be not more than 20 per cent of the borrower's annual income and to be payable in monthly installments.

j. Personal loans secured by new or used automobiles, provided that the loans on new automobiles shall not exceed ninety per cent of the dealer's cost of the car and loans on used automobiles shall not exceed the loan value stipulated for such cars in the Guide Book of the National Automobile Dealers' Association. Loans on used cars shall be repayable within twelve months, and loans on new cars within fifteen months.

k. Loans may be made to appliance and equipment dealers, secured by purchase contracts, provided that on non-recourse paper, the dealer shall maintain a reserve of not less than five per cent to protect the bank against losses on such paper.

1. Commodity loans secured by warehouse receipts in bonded warehouses or by field warehouse receipts of warehouse companies approved by the Directors' Loan Committee. Such commodity loans shall have an ample margin of safety and the lending officer must make certain that the property securing the loan is amply protected from all reasonable hazards by insurance or other satisfactory means.

m. Loans secured by a chattel mortgage on beef or dairy cattle. The herds securing any such loans shall be inspected, appraised, and approved by an appraiser approved by the Directors' Loan Committee. Such loans shall not exceed sixty-six and two-thirds per cent of the appraised value of the cattle securing the loan, and shall be for a term of not more than two years.

n. FHA Title I modernization loans may be made direct to the borrower or purchased from local contractors and their sources of supply.

o. The trade area of this bank shall be considered as the following counties in this state: Washington, Adams, Jefferson. Generally speaking, the lending activities of this bank shall be limited to borrowers residing in, or conducting enterprises in the above trade area. Loans to persons or firms outside of the said area, or secured by tangible property located outside of the said area shall be specifically approved by the Directors' Loan Committee.

8. Loans of the following type are not considered desirable loans for the purposes of this bank, and will ordinarily be declined unless specifically approved by the Directors' Loan Committee for reasons which appear to justify an exception to the bank's general policy:

a. Capital loans to a business enterprise where the loan cannot be repaid within a reasonable period except by borrowing elsewhere or by liquidating the business.

b. Loans to a new enterprise, if the repayment of the loan is dependent upon the profitable operation of the enterprise.

c. Loans to parties whose integrity or honesty is questionable.

d. Loans, the repayment of which is solely dependent upon the successful marketing of a growing crop.

e. Real estate mortgage loans secured by property located outside of the bank's recognized trade area.

f. Construction mortgage loans except in cases where the building is being supervised by a competent architect and the contractor has provided a performance bond, with acceptable surety, and the borrower has produced a satisfactory takeout commitment.

g. Loans secured by an assignment against an undistributed estate.

h. Loans secured by stock in a closed corporation which has no ready market.

i. Unsecured loans to individual members of the Board of Directors.

j. Loans for the purpose of enabling the borrower to speculate on the future market of securities or commodities.

k. "Accommodation Loans" will not be made to poor credit risks on the strength of a good endorser. If the loan will not "stand on its own feet," the loan should be made to the endorser, and the endorser allowed to make a loan to the person whom he wishes to accommodate.

9. As a general policy, all loans should have a plan of liquidation at the time they are made and the liquidating plan shall be stated in writing and filed in the credit file.

10. A written application should be prepared for all loans, in order that the bank will have a written record of the representations upon which the loan was based. The signature of the borrower on the application may be waived by lending officers at their discretion.

11. Interest rates shall be in accordance with the schedule adopted by the Directors' Loan Committee. The Directors' Loan Committee shall review the interest schedule not less frequently than once each ninety days for appropriate changes.

12. All unsecured loans in excess of $500.00 shall be supported by a financial statement signed by the borrower,

or prepared and certified by a public accountant.

13. It shall be the duty of the manager of the Credit Department to see that an appropriate memorandum is made for the credit file by the lending officer on each loan that is made. The memorandum shall recite the circumstances under which the loan was made, the factors which justified it, and the borrower's plan for repayment.